FINCHLEY AND WHETSTONE PAST

First published 2001
by Historical Publications Ltd
32 Ellington Street, London N7 8PL
(Tel: 020-7607 1628 Fax: 020-7609-6451)

ISBN 0 948667 75 3
British Library Cataloguing-in-Publication Data
A catalogue record for this book is available from the British Library

Typeset in Palatino by Historical Publications Ltd
Reproduction by G & J Graphics, London EC2
Printed in Zaragoza, Spain by Edelvives

The Illustrations
The following have kindly supplied illustrations:

Roger Cline: *15, 20, 23, 28, 29, 30, 100, 182*
John Heathfield: *1, 2, 18, 36, 37, 38, 39, 41, 43, 50, 51, 55, 56, 57, 58, 59, 61, 62, 63, 65, 66, 72, 76, 80, 85, 88, 90, 92, 103, 104, 116, 118, 119, 122, 123, 126, 129, 133, 135, 137, 138, 139, 145, 149, 152, 153, 154, 155, 156, 163, 166, 169, 171, 172, 178, 183*
Percy Reboul: *3, 4, 5, 6, 7, 8, 9, 11, 12, 13, 14, 16, 19, 21, 22, 24, 25, 27, 31, 32, 34, 35, 40, 42, 45, 46, 47, 49, 52, 53, 54, 64, 67, 68, 69, 70, 71, 73, 75, 77, 78, 81, 82, 84, 87, 89, 93, 94, 95, 96, 97, 98, 99, 101, 102, 105, 106, 107, 108, 109, 110, 111, 114, 115, 120, 121, 125, 127, 128, 130, 131, 132, 134, 136, 140, 142, 143, 144, 146, 147, 148, 150, 157, 158, 160, 161, 162, 164, 165, 167, 168, 170, 173, 174, 175, 176, 177, 179, 180, 181, 184, 185, 187*
The London Borough of Barnet Archives: *jacket illustration*
Historical Publications: *10, 26, 33, 44, 48, 60, 74, 79, 83, 91, 112, 113, 117, 124*

FINCHLEY AND WHETSTONE PAST

with Totteridge and Friern Barnet

John Heathfield
with an introduction by Percy Reboul

HISTORICAL PUBLICATIONS

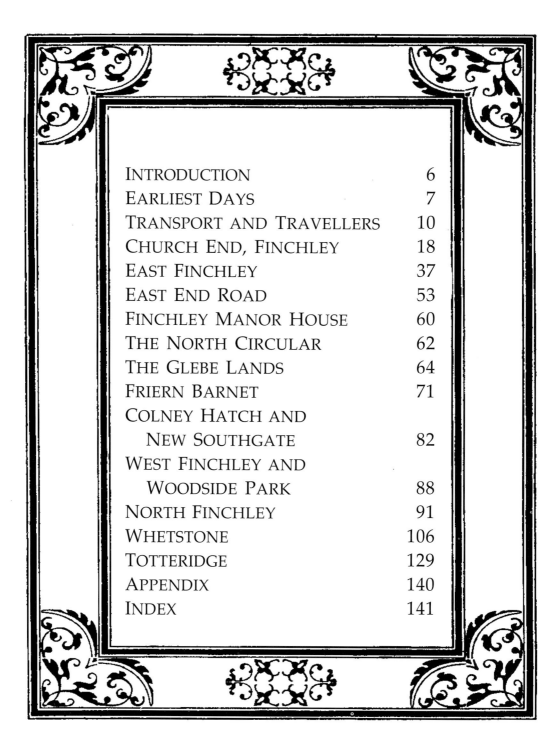

INTRODUCTION 6

EARLIEST DAYS 7

TRANSPORT AND TRAVELLERS 10

CHURCH END, FINCHLEY 18

EAST FINCHLEY 37

EAST END ROAD 53

FINCHLEY MANOR HOUSE 60

THE NORTH CIRCULAR 62

THE GLEBE LANDS 64

FRIERN BARNET 71

COLNEY HATCH AND
NEW SOUTHGATE 82

WEST FINCHLEY AND
WOODSIDE PARK 88

NORTH FINCHLEY 91

WHETSTONE 106

TOTTERIDGE 129

APPENDIX 140

INDEX 141

Acknowledgements

and references for further reading

The *Victoria County History* of Middlesex volume no. 6, published in 1970, is the most comprehensive study of our district. In particular it contains details of the lords of the various manors in considerable detail. It is available for reference at the Barnet Borough Archives, Egerton Gardens, Hendon.

The Archives, too, contain a mass of further information. Much of this was collected by C.O. Banks in the 1930s. He was a meticulous transcriber and many books written since his time have been a rehash of his work. Back copies of the *Finchley Press* and *Barnet Press* are accessible on micro film at Hendon and Chipping Barnet libraries. Copies of the rate books and minutes of council meetings are also available.

Fred Davis has written two useful books based on the researches of Banks. They are *The Finchley Charities* published by the Charities and *Finchley Common* published by Barnet Libraries.

W.E. Cowley researched the history of Totteridge. His unpublished papers are shared between the borough's archives, Hertfordshire Record Office and Barnet Museum.

The Totteridge Manor Association also has a good collection

.

Books consulted have included:
The Book of Totteridge by Diana Griffith, beautifully illustrated (published privately 1992).
'Local plays' by Bill Gelder (published privately 1976).
A short history of Totteridge in the county of Hertford, by Stanley G.R. Barratt (1934)
Henry Stephens, a centenary biography by Diana Young (published privately 1998)
A Place in Time, published by the Hendon & District Archaeological Society (1991)
The Dictionary of National Biography

I warmly acknowledge the help given by
Graham Bird of Barnet Education Department
Norman Burgess of the Finchley Society
Joanna Corden
John Donovan, of Friern Barnet Local History Society
Adrian Kosner
Basil McKenny of the Whetstone Society
Percy Reboul
Pamela Taylor

Introduction - the wider perspective

Encouraged by excellent television and radio programmes, there has developed in recent years a growing interest in genealogy, archaeology and local history. What was once the province of academics and professionals has become the hobby and even the passion of ordinary people.

Typically interest in the past often stems from curiosity about one's own family or house. From there it is but a short step to investigate the locale and borough with all their complexities. The past begins to call. The possibilities are endless!

Behind every part of the story lies our fascination with change. The major changes, the ones that affect us all, stem from national and international political decisions. The post-war National Health Service and social security schemes, for example, transformed the health of the nation. We no longer see suffering and death caused by diseases like diphtheria, whooping cough and polio. Neither do we see the huge infant mortality that was such a feature of Victorian and Edwardian London. Paradoxically our increasing affluence has brought its own big killers - heart disease, strokes, obesity and lung cancer. Our love affair with the car has resulted in hopelessly congested streets and an appalling number of deaths and serious injuries. In Friern Barnet, to quote just one statistic, there were more people killed on the roads during the last war than were killed by German bombs.

The beautiful countryside of this part of Middlesex which, a hundred years ago, brought walkers and cyclists from London to sample its delights, has disappeared. The fields and farms that at one time provided hay and dairy products for the capital have been replaced by houses, factories and roads. But however much we may regret the passing of a way of life, for most people it has been an improvement.

Another great change has been in the field of entertainment. Our Victorian forebears enjoyed the delights of Barnet Fair, local concerts and dramatic clubs, church outings, debating societies and the like. There was entertainment at home with parties followed by the party pieces of all those present. For many working class men there were the dubious delights of the pub. Drunkenness was rife. The role of the wife was mostly at home looking after the latest addition to an already large family.

The next 75 years saw a total transformation. For very little money people could enjoy the cinema and with the coming of radio, entertainment became based in the home. By 1937 public service television had been introduced, though reception was restricted to just a few miles from Alexandra Palace. This was taken out of service during the war, but since that time has become the major source of entertainment and education throughout the country. There must be people in the borough who saw the earliest aeroplanes fly at Hendon and yet have lived long enough to have seen on television men landing on the moon and close up views of the planets.

When we consider the benefits of today's 'essentials' – the deep-freeze, refrigerator, washing machine, vacuum cleaner etc., – the thought occurs "how did they manage?" The answer is "very well". On modest means people could afford a servant to do the menial work. In the 1920s and '30s the domestic telephone was comparatively rare, but there were numerous public telephone boxes and a telegraph service which delivered a message almost anywhere within a couple of hours. Labour was cheap for those who had the money to pay for it, and there were many people unemployed. In our district what few jobs were available locally were centred on farming and domestic work, but with the development of railways, both overground and later the Underground, people could travel easily for the first time to find employment outside the district.

Trams reinforced this mobility and the district was transformed. In 1901 there was a population of 76,000 in what is today's London Borough of Barnet, but the 1991 census shows one of 294,000, 54% of whom work outside the borough and one third of whom are employed in a managerial or professional capacity.

In 1935 religious establishments in the districts covered by this book included 13 Church of England, 4 Baptist, 1 Strict Baptist, 5 Congregational, 1 Jewish, 3 Methodist, 1 Presbyterian, 5 Catholic, 1 Unitarian and 1 Inter-denominational. There were also 25 other missions and religious associations. Attendance at evensong at Anglican churches regularly exceeded 600 and many churches had balconies added to cope with overcrowding.

It is possibly just this change in ethnic composition that would have caused most surprise to our predecessors. Early school photographs show very few other ethnic groups. The 1991 census however reveals that 22% of our residents were not born in the United Kingdom. The quality of race relations in the district, while not perfect, is a tribute to all concerned and there is widespread recognition of the resulting multicultural richness and diversity.

Percy Reboul

Earliest Days

GEOLOGY

The last ice age probably ended about 25,000 years ago. What was to become the borough of Barnet was covered by a sheet of ice which pushed a glacial moraine in front of it. The ice sheet reached about as far as East Finchley and the ridge running roughly east-west from Muswell Hill through Finchley to Hendon is partly formed by the debris left behind when it melted.

The ice sheet carried with it stones and boulders which it had picked up. These were scraped along the underlying bed rock with great force and the tiny, impervious particles thus formed, each smaller than a molecule of water, formed a dense layer of boulder clay.

As the ice melted it formed streams and rivers. The stones knocked against each other chipping off fragments, some of which were rounded by

1. A geological map of the borough of Barnet.

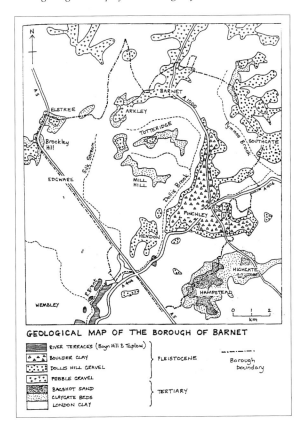

being tossed and turned in the current. Other fragments remained to form sand. The remains of these sand and gravel beds, characterised by round pebbles and known as Dollis Gravel, can be found at Hadley, Church Hill in East Barnet, Totteridge and the ridge where the High Road runs from Finchley to Whetstone.

Whetstone High Road is on a ridge of glacial gravel some ten metres thick. There are springs and streams emerging from the places where the gravel meets the underlying clay, which is the predominant feature of Whetstone's soil, as the local gardeners know to their cost. Just to the west of the High Road is a narrow band of Greensand running north-south, roughly along the line of the railway.

The subsequent history of our district was governed by its geology and topography. The great mass of low-lying heavy and wet clay soil eventually formed Finchley Common and the valleys and ridges became natural routes. Eventually, the close proximity to London ensured that once access was easy housing development would follow.

Sea shells of some sixty different species (possibly 75 million years old) dating from the Cretaceous period were discovered in the 1850s during the excavation of the railway cutting between New Southgate and Oakleigh Park stations. In 1895 animal bones, later identified as mammoth, elephant, hippo and rhino were discovered north of the Silk Bridge in Colindeep Lane, Hendon.

THE STONE AGE

The wide scatter of the few Old Stone Age finds suggests that the district was sparsely occupied by travelling hunter-gatherers at that time: the heavy soil and dense woodland would have made it unattractive for permanent settlement.

There was a concentration of finds at West Heath, Hampstead, arguably London's most important Middle Stone Age site. This was the subject of a major excavation by the Hendon and District Archaeological Society (HADAS). Some New Stone Age material has also been found, with the suggestion of a possible concentration near Brockley Hill. It is more likely however that this concentration of finds reflects the larger number of people observing rather than the degree of habitation.

A flint tool which was found at no. 69 Buckingham Avenue, Whetstone in 1946 seems to have disappeared

THE IRON AGE

There are two possible Iron Age earthworks in the borough. One is at Hadley and the other at Moat Mount, Hendon. Evidence about both is scant. A Gaulish coin was reported to have been found "near Barnet", but there have been few other finds, again probably reflecting a lack of seekers as much as an absence of inhabitants.

THE ROMAN PERIOD

Troops from the Claudian invasion of AD43 must have passed through our district. The most obvious Roman influence however is Watling Street, the great Roman road from London to St Albans, which survives as the Edgware Road.

Close to Watling Street is Brockley Hill. Early in Roman times the proximity of a good road, clay, sand, running water and wood for fuel from the nearby woods often led to the creation of an important pottery – the ruins of a number of kilns have been discovered by HADAS. No evidence of habitations has been found but finds of imported jewellery, glass and pottery, including Samian ware found nearby, suggest that there are Roman houses waiting to be found. No doubt there are also Roman tracks and side roads to be discovered.

The authoritative *A Place in Time*, published by HADAS in 1991, comments "We know as little about the end of Roman Barnet as we do about the beginning". After the Romans left, our district became a kind of border area at a time when the country was separated into small kingdoms, notably that of the East Saxons (whose boundaries seem to have run from the Thames to the Chilterns), Wessex and Mercia. Our district was probably part of Wessex by the year 825. Some fifty years later the kings of Wessex were acknowledged to be kings of all the English except in those areas occupied by the Vikings and Danes. In 1011 the *Anglo-Saxon Chronicle* records that the Viking bands which attacked London went "everywhere in flocks and harried our miserable people and robbed and slew them" – perhaps this included our district.

EARLY BOUNDARIES

Of particular significance is a group of charters from the cartulary of St Albans abbey discovered by Simon Keynes.

The abbey was given lands and money about the year 793 by Offa, King of Mercia. A document dated 1005 records the gift by King Aethelred of land, including Barnet, to the Abbot of St Albans. The boundary between Barnet and what became Friern Barnet is delineated as:

> From Bettstyle along the bishop's boundary to Wakeling Moor and then to Aggangeat, past a spit of land to the Brent, across that brook along the ditch to the boundary of Totteridge and then to Grendel's Gate.

Bettstyle still exists at the junction of Oakleigh Road South, Bowes Road and Brunswick Park Road. It was probably 'Betta's Stygle' – 'Stygle' is an old word for an animal enclosure and survives in modern English as 'sty' as in pig sty. Wakeling Moor is probably the low-lying damp ground near Sycamore Close off Longmore Avenue.

Aggangeat was near the junction of Northumberland Road and the Great North Road. 'Geat' or 'gate' implies the existence of a road, possibly leading to some kind of settlement at the top of Barnet Hill.

It seems that even before the Norman conquest what was to become Friern Barnet was separate from Barnet. Today's boundary follows almost exactly that delineated a thousand years ago. Possibly the Finchley boundaries had been settled by that period as well, though there is no

2. John Norden's map of 1760 showing Finchley and the surrounding district.

evidence for this before the thirteenth century.

Similarly the mention of Totteridge implies the existence of some kind of settlement there a thousand years ago.

The Bishop of London claimed what became Friern Barnet in 1187 and then granted it to the Knights Hospitaller in 1199. The Bishop also held what became Hornsey and Finchley and because he owned them both there was little need for him to spell out a clear boundary between them. The Bishop's hunting park, in existence by 1226, ran from Highgate and merged with Hornsey on the east. Northwards it ran about as far as Cherry Tree Woods and what is now the junction of Bishop's Avenue and Aylmer Road.

The Bishop's early records suggest that Finchley Manor formed part of the 50 hides shown in the Domesday Survey of 1086 that were owned by Fulham. In 1294 the Bishop claimed that his predecessors had owned Finchley 'from time out of mind' and it has indeed been suggested that Finchley was part of the land granted by Tyrhtel, Bishop of Hereford to Wealdheri, Bishop of London about 704.

The church at Finchley is first mentioned in 1274, that of Totteridge about 1250 and Friern Barnet's in 1199. This fits the pattern that most parishes had become established by the thirteenth century, though many had followed Saxon land boundaries.

FINCHLEY COMMON

Finchley Common ran roughly south to north from about where East Finchley Northern line station stands, past Totteridge Lane to the county boundary at Whetstone, and west to east from Dollis Brook to Muswell Hill. It was the property of the lord of the manor, that is to say in early times the Bishop of London. By the time of the Enclosure Act of 1816 it covered about 900 acres, but had previously been larger and had been called Finchley Wood. The soil was heavy clay and so both badly drained and very difficult to cultivate, although some of the higher parts were used for grazing. Such trees as existed were cut down partly to supply building materials but also for firewood since at that time all meals were cooked over a wood fire – the story of Little Red Riding Hood going into the woods to pick up sticks is based on practice. Evidence of grazing survives in place names like Grass Farm, Mutton Brook or Sheephouse Farm and others like Woodside and Woodhouse are reminders of a vanished woodland. Small patches of the original Middlesex forest survive in places such as Coldfall Wood, Cherry Tree Woods and Hollickwood.

Rights of Common were restricted to certain named commoners, so called because they held rights to use the land for grazing, collecting firewood etc. There are records of trespassers grazing animals on the Common without permission and a Common Driver or Drover was appointed to ensure that the rules were kept. In April 1693, for example, Richard Sutton of St Pancras was fined £10 "for driving and putting sheep and cattle to Common in Finchley, contrary to the custom of the said Manor".

Because the Common was so unattractive to cultivators it remained a great muddy obstacle until the coming of the railways and early settlements were around its edge.

Finchley Common was finally enclosed by Act of Parliament in 1816 and its land allotted to the commoners who had to 'enclose' it by means of hedge or fence within three months. In order to pay for the administration of the Act, certain lands were sold off. Thirty-four acres were bought by Thomas Collins of Woodhouse for £2,865 and 105 acres near Strawberry Vale went to the Regent's Canal Company for £9,366. The lord of the manor received 96 acres and the rector of St Mary's church got 117 acres.

Although Friern Barnet did not have a common as such, the soil conditions were such that much of Friern Barnet was undeveloped as indeed was Totteridge.

Transport and Travellers

The development of the whole district was dependent upon the early road system. There were at least two early routes north from the City of London. One went via Islington and the Holloway Road and then via 'Tallington Lane' to Crouch End, Muswell Hill and Colney Hatch to Friern Barnet. Another was up today's York Way, Brecknock Road and Dartmouth Park Hill and via Hornsey Lane to Crouch End. Both these routes were hilly and difficult in winter and were devious in direction. But at the end of the thirteenth century there was an improvement when the Bishop of London constructed a toll road across his park, beginning at what became the Gatehouse public house at Highgate, and going through Finchley and Whetstone and on to Barnet. This route became known as the Great North Road. There was also an old east-west route from Totteridge through Whetstone to Edmonton, which was called Avernstreet by 1499.

Maintenance of local paths and trackways was historically the responsibility of either manor or parish, but the main roads, such as the Great North Road, were deemed to be 'King's highways'. So out of repair had they become in the sixteenth century that the Highways Act of 1555 was brought in to put in place a system of maintenance. Each parish was required to elect two unpaid parishioners to inspect the main roads – in our case the Great North Road – and to supervise the labour forcibly supplied by inhabitants of the parish.

Needless to say, a system which relied extensively on unpaid and grudgingly given labour was unsatisfactory, especially with the growth of wheeled transport in the seventeenth century which made the roads even worse. During the eighteenth century many roads were effectively privatised, given over by Acts of Parliament to trusts which made their profits (if any) by charging tolls at turnpike gates on the routes they maintained. In our area eight miles of the road from the present-day junction of North Hill, Highgate and the Archway Road to Gannick Corner south of Potters Bar were taken over in

3. Changing the mail coach horses at the White Lion on the Great North Road in 1825.

1712 by the Whetstone and Highgate Turnpike Trust which produced what was said to be the finest eight-mile stretch of road in the kingdom.

There were turnpike gates at the southern end of the road, at Whetstone, at the foot of Barnet Hill and at Gannick Corner. There were complaints that the tolls were higher than those in adjoining toll roads and in 1806 the keeper of the Whetstone weighbridge was dismissed for letting his friends through at a reduced rate. The Whetstone toll gate was demolished in 1863 though a gate near the White Lion in East Finchley was still visible in 1901.

Finchley Road, Regent's Park Road and Ballards Lane are the names of different stretches of a new road built in 1825 by the St Marylebone and Finchley Turnpike Trust, which replaced the earlier winding roads on a similar route. There was a tollgate at the junction with East End Road. Ballards Lane joined the Great North Road at what became Tally Ho Corner.

The proximity to London produced traffic which in turn supported inns, livery stables, blacksmiths, wheelwrights and similar trades.

About 1815, 140 coaches a day were said to pass the Whetstone Turnpike. The first time-tabled stage coach (so called because the horses were changed at each stage) along the Great North Road was in 1637. For example in 1839 there was a conveyance to the Bank of England three times daily starting at the Bull Inn, Whetstone.

Coaches through Finchley to London in 1839 included:

The Criterion – Godden's Offices in Barnet at 9.00 am;

The Wonder – Old Salisbury Arms 5.00 pm, Sunday 6.00pm;

Elwood's Omnibus – Cock Inn Barnet 8.00 am and 7.00 pm;

Salmon's Omnibus – the Albion Barnet 9.00 am;

Ellis' Coaches – Queens Head, Finchley Common (Jas Love) dep. 8.45 am;

Robinson's – Torrington Arms (Geo Osman) 8.30 am;

Phillip Smith's omnibus – Five Bells (Richard Wisdom) 9.30 am;

Carriers carts – Jas Drewell and P Haughton. The journey to London took about 1½ hours.

Gravel was dug locally to surface the road and there were large gravel pits in Whetstone on what is now Swan Lane Open Space and on the Finchley Glebe Lands.

THE WHETSTONE AND HIGHGATE TURNPIKE TRUST

The accounts of the Trust for 1818-19 include:

Amount of mortgage debt @ 0.65%	£1,300
Annual produce of tolls	£3,700
Expense of repairing the road	£3,114
Ballast	£7,018

Labourers employed: 22 in winter, 16 in summer, exclusive of ballast diggers.

In 1833 Whetstone Gate was let for £7,350 per annum. This compares with 1794 when the takings were only £150 and indicates the great increase in stagecoach and other traffic at the beginning of the nineteenth century

Thomas Telford (1757-1834) rode the whole length of the road and wrote this report in 1819:

"All gravel is sifted over the fields, the second time in order to make it clean from sand and clay. The largest ballast upon the crown, the smallest upon the sides of the road. A cross drain every 4 yards and a good drain the whole length.

From Barnet Hill heading south.

Descending: General good form, surface loose. Bottom of hill, harder surface, heaps of gravel left side.

10 miles: *[Foot of Barnet Hill]* General good form, surface good, sides cleaned out, gravel heaps at side.

9 miles: *[now next to Ivy House Whetstone]* sides repaired with gravel. Pass Toll gate. Road repaired with gravel. Many gravel heaps.

8 miles: *[now outside Sainsbury's Finchley]* General from good, surface good, gravel right side, footpath left side

7 miles: *[now Fallow Corner, Granville Road]* ditto 2 men riddling gravel."

Road tolls varied from trust to trust.

Those for the gates on the Great North Road route for 1808 were:

	Galley	Sth Mimms	Whetstone
Coach & 6	9d	1s 6d	1s 0d
Coach & 4	6d	1s 0d	8d
Coach & 2	4½d	6d	4d
1 horse chaise	1½d	6d	2d
Horse	1d	1d	1d
Oxen per score	5d	6d	5d
Cart or wagon	1½d	6d	9d

The last meeting of the Trust was on 31 October 1863, when the only surviving trustee was Joseph Baxendale.

STAGE COACHES

Keeping and changing horses for the coaches was big business. Coldharbour in Whetstone High Road, (now EMC Advertising) was an early coaching inn described in 1701 as having "good stables and a brew house". It was owned by William Castle, a horse dealer, in 1784; in 1790 it was sold to John Kendrick, a horse dealer from Kilburn, who also exported horses to France.

Peter Mountain had extensive stables in Whetstone High Road with a small coach repair workshop about where Waitrose now stands. His widow Ann Mountain is shown in Pigot's Directory of 1832 living in Whetstone. Mountain's coaches ran from the Saracen's Head in Snow Hill in London.

Joseph Baxendale of Whetstone took over the ailing firm of Pickford Brothers about 1817. In the 1820s he acquired the business of Francis Choppin, a bankrupt horse dealer, and in 1836 took over the large concern of Chaplin & Horne.

Benjamin Horne had stables at the White Lion, Finchley and William Chaplin had stabling for 82 horses at the Swan and Pyramids and further stabling behind the Park Road Hotel (at today's Tally Ho Corner), including accommodation for the Tally Ho coach which ran from London to Birmingham. Chaplin had about 2,000 horses and 27 stage coaches leaving London every night. In 1851, Pickford's employed 7 stable keepers, 4 horse buyers, 17 grooms, a jockey, 19 smiths and several harness makers.

OMNIBUSES AND TRAMS

In 1884 H. Newman had a 4-horse omnibus which left the Salisbury Arms, Barnet for Finchley and London daily at 12.30, 1.30, 6.30 and 8pm. Other local omnibuses connected Barnet, Whetstone and Church End, Finchley in 1898. A service from the Bald Faced Stag to Euston and the East End of London ran every 15 minutes in 1899. In 1905 the London General Omnibus Company opened a horse-drawn route from the Bald Faced Stag to St Martin's Lane in the West End, but by 1908 motor buses were running from North Finchley to Oxford Circus every 15 minutes.

4. The Tally Ho London to Birmingham coach at speed.

5. *A horse bus to the Bank of England outside the Torrington, North Finchley.*

6. *A North Finchley to Oxford Street omnibus. They ran every 15 minutes.*

It was the coming of electric trams that made the centre of London accessible as a place of employment for the poor of our district. The vehicles' large capacity and cheap fares, especially the reduced 'workmen's rate' before 8am, were crucial in this process, just as they had been in the spread of local railways.

Metropolitan Electric Tramways (MET) opened route 19 from Highgate to Whetstone in 1905 and extended it to the top of Barnet Hill in 1907. Service 21 worked from Tally Ho corner to Holborn via New Southgate and Wood Green from 1909. Trams from Barnet through Golders Green to Harlesden and Willesden were introduced at the same time – this became route 45. Route 60 ran in a semi-circle from North Finchley through Willesden to Paddington. The trams from Golders Green crossed over the path of the trams to Highgate near Percy Road in Finchley High Road – a potential site for a collision.

The MET bought a site for their Finchley depot in 1904 and a new road, Rosemont Avenue, had to be built to service it. The depot opened on 7 June 1905 with accommodation for sixty tramcars. Extra land was bought in 1907 and an extension in 1912 had a frontage on the Great North Road but no access.

Alterations were made in 1930-31 to cater for longer trams and further alterations were needed in August 1936 when trolleybuses were introduced. There was eventually room for 100 buses.

From November 1961 trolleybuses were gradually replaced by Routemaster diesel-engined buses and the last trolleybus ran from the depot on 2 January 1962. The site of the depot is now a Homebase store.

The increase in traffic and the danger caused by trams changing tracks at Tally Ho Corner led to the decision to cut a new road in 1934 called Kingsway from Woodhouse Road west to Ballards Lane and bring in a one way system round North Finchley. The previous extension of Nether Street to the High Road became the main bus stand.

Trams were replaced by trolleybuses as far as North Finchley in 1936 and up to Barnet in 1938. On the whole the route numbers remained identifiable. For example tram route 21 became the 621 trolley bus. Perhaps the shortest-lived route was number 651 which ran for 77 days between 6 March and 31 May 1938 from Barnet church via Finchley to Golders Green.

There was a considerable amount of affection for trams, as evidenced in 'last journey' ceremonies and celebrations on various routes around

7. *Regent's Park Road c.1905 illustrating three modes of horse-drawn transport.*

8. *An electric tram outside Regent's Parade, Ballards Lane, Finchley.*

London. According to the *Barnet Press*, London Transport obligingly arranged for the driver and conductor of the first tram from Barnet in 1907 to take charge of the last tram on 3 August 1938. They were Mr W. Lowe of 34 Kingsmead, Barnet and Mr F. Mardell of 34 Lambert Road, Finchley. At midnight conductor Mardell gave the signal to start. Nothing happened. The old tram apparently overcome with emotion refused to leave

9. *Trolley bus passing the Gaumont North Finchley at the junction of the High Road and Woodhouse Road.*

Barnet. A practical joker had cut the signal rope.

When the tram eventually reached Finchley, followed by dozens of motorists sounding their horns, fervour broke out. Sections of the crowd sang *Poor Cock Robin* and *Dear Old Pals* and others danced impromptu waltzes on the pavement. The tram was in complete darkness when it arrived because apparently souvenir hunters had taken all the light bulbs. Not only did Mardell have to issue tickets to an enormous crowd, many of whom were not able actually to have a ride, but he was also kept busy signing autographs.

In their turn trolleybuses were phased out between 1959 and 1962 (but without speeches of affection!). Apparently the London Passenger Transport Board bus services were so poor between 1959 and 1964 that Finchley Borough Council considered starting its own service.

THE RAILWAYS

The main line railway from King's Cross to Scotland skirted Muswell Hill and ran north. A station was built to service Colney Hatch Asylum which had its own gas works and supplied the railway station with water and gas before the establishment of the Colney Hatch Gas Light and Coke Company. It was originally planned to call the station Betstyle but it was named Colney Hatch & Southgate when it opened, and Southgate & Colney Hatch in 1860. It was inadequate, and in 1854 £450 had to be spent on improvements. In 1860 half the carriage shed was converted into a waiting room for passengers and accommodation for holding cattle was provided. The down sidings were lengthened the same year when a builder's yard was opened nearby. There were further additions in 1892.

There was also a special siding leading into the Great Northern Cemetery, so that funeral parties (and the deceased) could arrive by train. The signal box called Cemetery Box at the south end of the tunnel survived until 1973.

Oakleigh Park Station was opened on 1 December 1873. An old footpath connecting Whetstone with East Barnet church was preserved when a bridge running from Oakleigh Park South was erected in 1873.

Plans for the Edgware, Highgate & London Railway were made in 1863. The line (from 1867 run by the Great Northern Railway) ran overground to Seven Sisters Road (now Finsbury Park), but there were engineering problems including a 13-arch viaduct crossing the Dollis Brook and two tunnels with nasty earth slips. The line was eventually opened on 22 August 1867. Local stations were called East End Finchley and, after two name changes, Finchley Church End (now Finchley Central) with a single line running to Mill Hill. An extension to Barnet with intermediate stations at Torrington Park and Totteridge was opened on 1 April 1872. The name Whetstone was added to the latter in 1874 and Torrington Park was changed to Woodside Park in 1882.

The last steam passenger train from Finsbury Park to High Barnet was the 10.47 p.m. on Saturday 20 April 1940. The first electric train had run on 6 April 1940.

It was the coming of the railway that caused the increase in housing in the district after 1870, but the construction of tram routes about 1905 led to a reduction in railway passenger traffic and so of receipts. There was a fall in the amount of money available to invest in the railways in the 1920s. In a sense the success of the railways led to their own downfall.

10. East Finchley station c.1905. It was opened as East End Finchley and became East Finchley in 1886.

11. *Finchley Central station, originally Finchley Church End.*

12. *Woodside Park station, originally Torrington Park.*

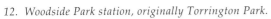

13. *The Broadway at Ballards Lane, Finchley, c.1904.*

Church End, Finchley

The name Finchley probably means 'Finch's clearing'. It may well be Anglo-Saxon although Finchley is not mentioned as such before the thirteenth century.

Early Finchley was mostly open common land with a few large estates and small settlements around the edges. There were three main centres of population or 'ends'. From the thirteenth century people were living at Church End (now central Finchley), East End is first mentioned in 1365 and North End became Whetstone.

Finchley developed along the route of what became the Great North Road, although that name was not used before about 1690. The southern part of the road from the Bishop's Gate near Highgate was called Newgate Lane in 1395 and the northern part Whetstone Streete in 1439. The central stretch was simply called the road to Barnet.

Other important early roads ran from Hendon to Church End, from Church End to East End and from Totteridge to Edmonton through Whetstone.

Hendon Lane is one of the oldest roads in the district. Other early names include Finchley Hill (1659) which may be the same as Alcokes Lane possibly from Alkokkes Field in 1365. Ducksetters Street or Lane ran from Golders Green to Hendon by 1475 – Walter Duck had a field nearby by 1365.

ST MARY'S CHURCH

St Mary, the parish church of Finchley in Hendon Lane, (mentioned in 1356), is basically a fifteenth century structure, built of ragstone rubble, though parts of it appear to be Norman and suggest an earlier building on the same site. The west tower is unbuttressed. Extensive restoration was carried out in 1872 when a south aisle was added by A. Billing; an outer side aisle to designs by Sir Charles Nicholson was added in 1932. The east end was damaged by bombing in 1940, but the whole building was restored again in 1950.

14. *Hendon Lane at the beginning of the 19th century. Clements' Nursery is in the foreground, the Manor Farm Dairy shop is to the right and Christ's College is in the distance.*

15. *St Mary's, parish church of Finchley. An engraving published in 1815.*

CHRIST'S COLLEGE

Opposite the church was Christ's College, designed by Anthony Salvin in 1857 and unkindly described as having a candle snuffer on top of the tower. It is built of purple brick with Tudor-style decoration in vitrified brick. It was opened for the pupils in 1860, though the official opening was not until July 1861. The buildings were extended in 1927.

The school had begun in 1857 with three pupils in what was grandly called 'Finchley Hall', but which had formerly been the Queen's Head pub (*see pp 22-3*). The moving spirit was the Revd Thomas Reader White, rector of St Mary's church. The number of pupils rose to 150 in three years because the large numbers of civil servants and officers in the armed forces who were serving abroad in Victorian times led to a demand for boarding school places which the school was able to meet. The 1881 census shows 52 boarders aged from 9 to 16 who were looked after by a matron, a wardrobe woman, a cook, seven housemaids and a scullery maid.

Finchley Hall continued to be used as a dormitory block until the 1890s.

The school was in financial difficulties throughout the 1890s and it was taken over in 1902 by

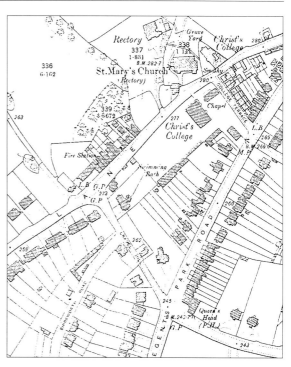

17. The centre of Church End in 1895, showing the parish church and Christ's College.

16. Christ's College in Hendon Lane in 1870. Their original building, called Finchley Hall, is partially hidden behind the tree. The boy on the barrow is thought to be the school caretaker's son.

18. *Christ's College officer cadet corps in c.1945.*

Middlesex County Council as the first County Grammar School and one of the first of such schools in England. The head master at that time was J.T. Philipson, a remarkable man and an outstanding educationalist whose legacy of inspiring the very highest standards has remained to this day. After his death in 1929, his successor was H.B. Pegrum who also served for some thirty years.

After the borough changed to the comprehensive system in 1976 there were plans in 1978 to combine Christ's College with Alder School to form Brooklands School and a new building was erected for about a thousand students in East End Road.

The old buildings were taken over by Pardes House and Beis Yaakov (Jewish) Primary Schools, though the girls' school was later moved to 373 Edgware Road.

FINCHLEY FIRE STATION

The row of shops in Hendon Lane just to the south of the church housed the fire station from 1888 until 1935. The fire service became professional in 1899 and in 1904 a Merryweather motorised fire engine was bought – this is now in the Science Museum.

There were sub-stations used to store a hand pump mounted on a cart, hoses and tools at Woodhouse Road and High Road, Whetstone. The latter building, a corrugated iron structure, still survives.

The junction of Hendon Lane and Regent's Park Road was occupied by William Clements' Nursery (*see ill. 14*) until about 1910, when it was moved further south. Clements was principally a florist but grew cash crops like lettuce and tomatoes. Holly Cottage on the corner of College Road was originally a shoeing forge.

19. *Finchley Fire Brigade c.1875.*

LOCAL GOVERNMENT

Parish government emerged gradually as population grew and affairs became more complicated. Meetings "for matters of the King as for the church and parish" were held at the Church House in 1547, though a 'rector's clerk' is mentioned as early as 1379. By 1561 the church and the clerk's house had become mingled with the estates of the Finchley Charities. By 1577 there were two wards called Finchley and Whetstone but by the late eighteenth century they were called East End and North End, presumably reflecting the changes in population pattern.

The various offices of Overseer of the Poor, Surveyor of the Highways, Ale Taster and Headborough (an early parish constable) were filled annually and were not popular with those appointed since they were unpaid and usually involved lots of paperwork. Anyone refusing to serve had to pay £10 to the parish and some were glad to do so. Rates to cover highway maintenance and the relief of the poor were levied twice a year at a full meeting of all parishioners.

Meetings were held in the vestry room of the church and from about 1718 at the Queen's Head, which stood about where the public library is

20. *The Barnet Press was founded by the Cowing family in June 1859. "We have no political axe to grind. We seek to record local life", stated F.W. Cowing in 1861. A separate Finchley edition was published from about 1880. In 1967, the rival Finchley Press was purchased. On the retirement of Jessica Cowing in 1957, the papers went into commercial management.*

now in Hendon Lane. The War Office Billeting Return of 1756 shows the pub with billets for two men and one horse, so it was quite small. Some of the vestry minute and account books from about 1780 survive, but many of the earliest records were lost when the Queen's Head was burned down in 1836. The building was re-erected and became Finchley Hall and used as a school (*see p 20*); it was bombed on 4 October 1940. A salaried collector of the Highway Rate was appointed in 1840 and a paid surveyor in 1856.

Finchley became an Urban District Council in 1895 when F. Goodyear was the first chairman. The council offices were at the rebuilt Finchley Hall, which was extended in the 1930s. After wartime bombing the council offices were moved to Avenue House (*see p27*).

Finchley became a borough on 5 October 1933 when the Earl of Athlone and Princess Alice, Countess of Athlone gave a Royal Charter to Alderman Vyvyan Wells, Finchley's first mayor. Wells was born in 1875 in Finchley, where his farmer grandfather Robert, had built Wentworth Park in 1805 on the site of the former Finchley Park. Wells, who had attended Christ's College, followed in the footsteps of his father, Henry, who had been the last chairman of the Finchley Local Board (1894) and the first chairman of the Urban District Council.

Vyvyan, christened Henry, adopted his name to avoid confusion with his father. He became a solicitor and in 1905 lived at Fir Cottage, Ballards Lane (nos. 53-55). He was appointed Clerk to the Finchley Charities in 1905 at salary of £25 p.a., which he served for 46 years. He was first elected to the Council in 1914, but he joined the army in 1918 and it was not until 1926 that he was re-elected. In 1928 he hosted a dinner given to celebrate the jubilee of Finchley becoming a UDC and was elected chairman. Two years after becoming the first mayor of Finchley, he was in 1935 the first person to receive the Freedom of the Borough of Finchley. In 1939 he sold Fir Cottage to the brewers so that they could enlarge the Joiner's Arms. He died in 1950 aged 75.

King Edward Hall, built in 1911, was used by the Borough Treasurer's department – the ground floor was taken for an adult lending library in 1945. The large hall on the second floor was used for dances and other functions. The site, on the corner of Ballards Lane and Hendon Lane, had previously been Clements' nursery.

BIBBESWORTH MANOR

Bibbesworth Manor to the west of Regent's Park Road, named after the family which once owned it, goes back to before 1319. In 1449 the estate consisted of 550 acres of land and woodland, six houses and properties in Finchley and Hendon. Land on the estate north of Gravel Hill was sold

21. The so-called 'Finchley Village' west of Hendon Lane, developed after 1910 in garden city style.

about 1840. Development southwards followed where Cyprus and Bibbesworth Roads existed by 1892; Allandale Avenue, Fitzalan and Arden Roads and Chessington Avenue were built by 1935. Salisbury Avenue was largely occupied by Clements' Nursery in 1935 (which had moved from Hendon Lane), and contained only five other houses. Haslemere, Fairholme and Kinloss Gardens were not developed until the 1950s.

The so called 'Finchley village' (*ill. 21*) to the west of Hendon Lane and to the east of the Dollis Brook, was developed after 1910. Inspired by the Hampstead Garden Suburb, it was built by the Finchley Co-partnership Society for the "less wealthy middle classes". It soon comprised Cyprus Avenue, Hendon Avenue, Claremont Park, Lyndhurst Road and Village Road.

COLLEGE FARM

Sheephouse Farm was to the south of the parish church. 97 acres, known as Hendon Lane Farm, were owned in 1843 by F.A. Hamilton who lived in Nether Street. Sir George Barham (1836-1913) bought Sheephouse Farm and renamed it College Farm in 1868. He had founded the Express Dairy in Bloomsbury in 1864 using the newly developed railways around King's Cross to bring milk to London - his trademark was an express train. He invented the first conical milk churn, made by another of his companies, the Dairy Supply Company. An outbreak of rindepest in 1865 led to the slaughter of all cows in the capital, but because the Express Dairy was bringing in its milk from the country it was able to sell it to the small London dairy farmers. Barham had studied dairying in the USA, India and Jamaica and had arranged for the import of pedigree cattle from Australia. The result in 1883 was a model farm at Finchley stocked with Jersey, Shorthorn and Kerry cattle. In 1882 Barham employed Frederick Chancellor to design new model dairy buildings. The architect's previous experience had been with churches and some of the buildings he designed for the dairy have a decidedly unusual appearance.

Barham rapidly became a public figure, arguing the case for the beneficial effects of fresh milk. It became customary for the dairy to supply a currant bun, a boiled egg or a slice of cake with every pint of milk, thus beginning the catering side of the business. By 1890 Express Dairy was

22. College Farm, formerly Sheephouse Farm, acquired by George Barham of Express Dairy in 1868.

23. *A miniature Dexter Kerry cow belonging to Express Dairy at Finchley, exhibited at an International Health Exhibition.*

24. *A bottling room at the College Farm dairy.*

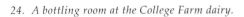

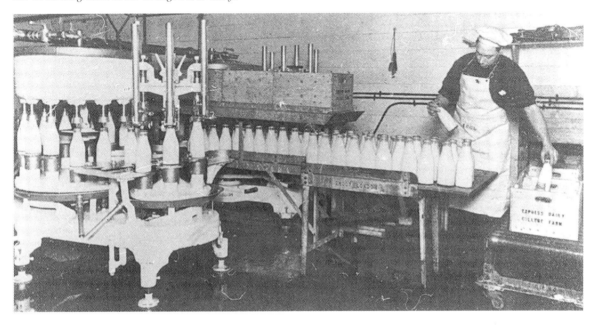

supplying the Queen with milk and obtained the royal warrant in 1895. Barham was knighted in 1904 and in 1905 was a member of a Royal Commission on milk and cream standards. Barham also had a short-lived "picturesque octagonal farm" at Kenwood in Highgate.

After his death his son Titus inherited the milk business and *his* son Arthur had the Dairy Supply Company, wholesale milk, catering and utensils. About 1918 the Dairy Supply Company merged with two other companies to become United Dairies (now Unigate). In 1921, College Farm became one of the first tuberculin tested dairies to be built. Express Dairies pulled out in 1972 and since that time the farm has been kept as a valuable educational and recreational resource run by a charity.

25. The late rurality of Finchley is here depicted in this 1934 picture of Mrs Lily Mortimer, a shepherdess whose flock grazed fields between East End Road and Hampstead Heath.

REGENT'S PARK ROAD

The construction of Regent's Park Road meant that the old roads lost their importance and a new centre sprang up at the junction with East End Road. A new pub (built in 1868) was called the Queen's Head replacing the building further to the west which had become the Finchley Hall (see above).

North of East End Road, The Avenue was constructed and planted with a lining of trees about 1604 in order to give the then lady of the manor, Mrs Elizabeth Kinge, a pleasant walk to St Mary's church.

Land near Avenue House was leased for building from 1864. Avenue House was actually built in 1867 but Henry C. Stephens, the famous ink manufacturer, bought its freehold in 1874 and built what Pevsner calls a "reactionary Italianate" house of some 60 rooms in 1884. His house, one of the first to be lit by electricity, is on what was Temple Croft field of some 40 acres, named from

26. The original trees in The Avenue were planted in 1604.

27. Avenue House, home of ink manufacturer H.C. Stephens and later to be used for local government offices.

28. A public library was established at Avenue House in 1933.

FINCHLEY PUBLIC LIBRARY

The Council are establishing at Avenue House, East End Road, N.3, a Public Library, embodying a small reference section, which will be available without fee to all who live, work, or study in Finchley.

◎

THE BOOKS, which may be borrowed for home reading, will include those by standard and classic authors, text-books and technical works, and, as far as is possible, the best work of modern writers.

THE SERVICE will place at the disposal of Finchley residents, through the agency of the National Central Library, the resources of almost every library of importance in the country. Every effort will be made to obtain for readers all books which come within the scope of a public library.

THE HOURS of opening will be from 10-30 a.m. to 1 p.m., and from 2 p.m. to 7-30 p.m. daily, except on Wednesdays and Sundays, when the Lending Library will be closed.

THE OFFICIAL DATE of opening by the Chairman of the Council (Councillor A. T. Pike, J.P.,) is Saturday, 28th October, 1933. The Library will be open to the public on the following Monday, 30th October.

H. WOOD BARTER,
Clerk of the Council.

Municipal Offices,
Finchley, N. 3.

the Templars who had owned the land in 1243. It was used as a hospital for airmen in World War One, and then retained for use by the Ministry of Health until 1925. By 1933 it accommodated the public library and was used as a Control Centre for Civil Defence in 1939. After the bombing of the council offices in 1940, local government activities were transferred to Avenue House and the former drawing room became the council chamber. The first officer's chair is still in the building.

Henry Stephens (born 1841) lived there until his death in 1918 – his nickname 'Inky' lives on. His father Charles had bought Grove House in Ballards Lane (about where Tesco's stands) where he made inks and dyes in a series of outhouses and sheds. Henry took control of the business in 1864 on the death of his father and his exceptional organising ability and brilliance as a chemist soon led to a huge expansion of the business. He entered Parliament as member for Hornsey but resigned after thirteen years over a difference of opinion with the government on the treatment of the Boers. At his death he was worth £279,000. He bequeathed Avenue House and ten acres of garden to the people of Finchley, but neglected to make any provision for their upkeep.

The house and grounds were formally opened to the public on 3 May 1928.

Avenue House now includes a small museum and archive run by the Finchley Society, which was formed to preserve Finchley's heritage. The president of the Finchley Society is the comedian, Spike Milligan.

Hertford Lodge, the building immediately to the west of Avenue House and used for many years as council offices, was built at about the same time as Avenue House. In 1892 it was occupied by John Heal (see below). In 1937 the house was used by the Misses MacDonald as a boarding and day school for boys and girls "assisted by a staff of visiting and resident mistresses".

Opposite Avenue House, land on the former Bibbesworth estate was built up from 1890. James and Ernest Vaughan laid out Stanhope and Cavendish Avenues in 1891-2. What were described as "superior semi-detached houses" were built along Regent's Park Road about 1900 and a parade of shops to service the estate followed about 1905. Windermere Avenue and Mountfield Road were made up in 1910 and Templars Crescent was built in the 1930s.

St Luke's Church in Mountfield Road opened in 1904, financed mostly by the parishioners. There was a grant from the Ecclesiastical Commissioners as well. The architect was W D Caröe. The church hall dates from 1937.

GRASS FARM AND DOLLIS BROOK

Grass Farm, one of the largest farms in Finchley, was west of the church, the site of what is now Dollis Park, Dollis Avenue, Lyndhurst Gardens, Grass Park and as far as the Hendon boundary at Dollis Brook. About 1856 it was bought by John Heal, a successful London designer and furniture shop owner, who asked Edward Roberts to design an entrance lodge in 1859. After his death in 1876, his widow Annie lived there until 1890. The Heal business, begun by John Harris Heal as a feather dresser in Rathbone Place off Oxford Street in 1810, moved to Tottenham Court Road in 1840, selling principally bedding but soon included bedsteads. There was a large expansion in 1875 to include other furniture.

The great-grandson of the firm's founder, Sir

29. *Dollis Brook, from a drawing by S.W. Clutton. The stream supplies water to the Welsh Harp reservoir in Brent.*

30. *A cigarette named after Finchley's local stream! A 1933 advertisement.*

31. A bridge across the Dollis Brook c.1904.

Ambrose Heal (1872-1959), introduced the appreciation of wood as a medium. His designs were based on simplicity and function. Antique furniture, kitchens, pottery, carpets, textiles and curtains, were added in the 1950s. Heal's was noted for quietness and good taste. Ambrose said that it was important to get rid of otiose decoration and produce good adornment to the home at affordable prices.

Frank Heal, who inherited the land at Finchley, sold some of it to James Williamson of Elm Grange in 1894. By 1906 Charles Day, a developer, was offering houses with 3 receptions and 6 bedrooms for £1,150. They were "Beautifully fitted and decorated, detached, with motor homes if required".

ST MARY'S SCHOOL

A 'villager' had commented in 1813 that no parish within 300 miles of London had more children in a deplorable state of ignorance than Finchley, an observation made at a time when some progress was being made. A Methodist Sunday School was begun about 1812 and St Mary's School was opened in 1813 occupying a building in Hendon Lane leased from the Finchley Charities. St Mary's was intended for 35 boys and 30 girls. Having received a grant from the National Society for the Education of the Poor in the Principles and Practice of the Established Church (note the capital letters), it became known as the National School. It moved to the corner of Hendon Lane and Victoria Avenue in 1848 and in 1864 there were two small classrooms for 67 boys and 32 girls. In 1905 a new infants' school was built on adjoining glebe land. The two schools were combined in 1933 and extra classrooms were added in 1949 and 1967. The whole school was removed to a new site in Dollis Park in April 1990 and its former site is now occupied by the County Court.

32. *St Mary's schools in Hendon Lane, c.1905. Christ's College is in the distance.*

BALLARDS LANE

The origin of the name Ballards Lane is obscure, but in 1323, Robert Pratt was found not guilty of robbing Henry Ballard of Finchley. This is the only record of the name in Finchley. In 1431 there is a mention of dirty ditches in Ballards Lane so the road is certainly very old. There are also references to Ballards Redynges and Ballards Redynges Gate – Redynge is a middle-English word for a clearing.

Like most other local roads, Ballards Lane was originally a muddy track winding from Tromers Street (John Tromer appeared at the Bishop's court in 1375 and is mentioned again in the Middlesex Court Records in 1401)) or Gravel Hill near the church to Angels Farm, which was near the present junction with Granville Road. Here the lane met the Moss Hall estate where it stopped. In the eighteenth century it was extended under the direction of Mr Brown, the parish surveyor, to meet the circuitous Nether Street at its junction with the Great North Road. In 1765 the Finchley Charities "paid Mr Brown towards the new raised way from the last house [Angels] in Barrow Lane to the Turnpike Road - £10".

James Williamson (*see p29*) set about developing the Elm Park Road estate on the northern side of the railway. It was slow to sell and by 1892

Gordon Road had only Oakdene, Rocklands and Nether Court, large Victorian houses with carriage sweeps at the front.

At Fallow Court in Nether Street lived Alderman Frederick Goodyear (1844-1937), a man typical of many unsung local politicians. He earned his money as a straw hat and clothing manufacturer. When he took his wife on honeymoon to Devon in 1867 for a three-week tour, he did so driving a pony and trap. He particularly disliked motor cars and must have been one of the last people in Finchley regularly to use a pony and trap for local travel. He served on the Finchley Local Board from 1882 where he was chairman of the Finance Committee and was a member of the first Finchley Urban District Council from 1895 till 1900. Later a county councillor, he was also a founder member of the Finchley Liberal Association. He was instrumental in the Middlesex County Council taking over Christ's College to become Finchley's first secondary school, thereby ensuring the survival of what became a first rate school remembered with affection by many former pupils.

The Railway Hotel (now the Ferret and Trouser leg!) on the corner of Ballards Lane and Nether Street, built 1869, obviously followed the opening of the station. It was rebuilt in 1962. Albert

33. *The Railway Hotel in Ballards Lane, c.1904. The pub was rebuilt in 1962.*

34. *The Old King of Prussia in Church End, c.1905.*

35. Watson's shop in the Broadway, Finchley c.1908.

Terrace was a row of seven shops running to the north. Around the corner at no. 3 Albert Place was Henry Hilsdon, a job master – that is, in 1892, he hired out ponies and traps for specific jobs and was the forerunner of today's minicab firms.

Grove House was the first house to be bought by the Stephens family (*see p 27*) – it is now remembered in the name of The Grove. Another large house in Ballards Lane was Falkland House, home in 1892 of Henry Hamilton.

Pope's Alley and Pope's garage stood at the northern end of what is now Tesco's (hence Pope's Drive). As well as running the garage, George Pope was part time Superintendent of the Fire Brigade. When Captain Scott went to the Antarctic in 1910 he took with him motorised sledges said to be equipped with Vauxhall engines fitted by Pope's. Unfortunately the intense cold froze the fuel system and the sledges were almost unusable.

Wentworth Lodge, built in 1828, occupied a very large tract of land between Ballards Lane and the railway. The Wentworth estate was originally laid out by the Conservative Land Society in 1868 in a bid here and elsewhere to increase the number of householders on voting registers who would vote for their party. However, mostly the streets were built from 1900 to 1910.

Cornwall House in Ballards Lane, together with its splendid bow window, still exists from about 1795. It was formerly called Selina Villa when it was owned by Joseph Thorley, a manufacturer of animal foods. Cornwall Avenue was built when the gardens of the house were sold about 1900. Amory's the printers, one of the district's oldest surviving firms, have a works complete with stables nearby built of yellow stock brick, dating from about 1900.

Across the road, Claverly was a large house owned by Edmund Hazlehurst and demolished to make Claverly Grove about 1900. Charles Day, the developer, offered houses on this estate at £325 to £400 – "The cheapest houses in Finchley".

The police station (1889) and nearby Finchley Meeting Hall were built on the Ballards Lane edge of the Wentworth estate.

The foundation stone for the Wesleyan Chapel is marked 1879. The architect was Charles Bell and the builder, J. Woodward. Benefactors included Alexandra Ladies' College in Alexandra Grove and Mrs Hamilton.

Gruneisen Road and Brownlow Road both date from about 1890. Essex Park, begun in 1880, derives its name from Essex House, the home of the Turner family, the site of which is now occupied by Fountains Court and Finchley Court (1935). Seymour Road, with many of its houses tile hung, and Etchingham Park were built on part of Fallow Farm by Frederick Wheeler about 1880. Etchingham Lodge, erected in 1878, was demolished to make space for Holdenhurst Road.

The foundation stone of St Paul's' church in Long Lane was laid by Mrs Hamilton of Brent Lodge and the building completed about 1885. A new parish was created for it out of St Mary's and Christ Church. The church, designed by John Ladds, is described as being in the Early English style with chancel, knave, aisles, transept and turret. It possesses a bell inscribed *Beatus venter qui te portavit* – literally 'Blessed be the womb that carried you'. Said to date from 1380, it was made by John Langhorne of London and originally hung at Hatford in Berkshire. The adjacent church hall was added in 1899. An oil bomb which fell into the organ in 1941 did not improve the tone.

The roads between the church and Finchley Central station all date from the end of the nineteenth century. Granville and Montrose Roads had been cut through the fields of Fallow Farm by 1890.

On the corner of Granville Road at 275 Ballards Lane stood the offices of the Finchley Conservative Association.

Margaret Thatcher was elected MP for Finchley in 1959. She was born in Grantham on 13 October 1925. Her talent was recognised early and she became a minister in 1961 – only the second woman to become a member of a Conservative cabinet. She was prime minister from 1979 until 1990, the first woman prime minister of a European country and the first British prime minister to win three consecutive terms. She was appointed OM in 1990 and a Baroness in 1992.

Mrs Thatcher arouses strong reactions. Her public persona appeared almost aggressive, perhaps because she was not afraid to take unpopular decisions. Those who were close to her as civil servants and in the local constituency party are united in their admiration for the care and consideration which she showed to them as individuals.

LOCAL CINEMAS

Finchley Meeting Hall was renamed the Wentworth Hall about 1900. It was the first building in Finchley to have rows of seats fixed to the floor so that patrons could view films. In that sense it is the first cinema in the district. In January 1910 it showed a "screamingly funny two reeler" called "Scroggins puts up for Blankshire", in which he has water thrown on him from an upstairs window whilst canvassing and has custard pies thrown at him during an election meeting. In the 1930s the Hall was used for billiards and is now a car showroom (*ill. 37*).

The Old Bohemia, described in the *Finchley Press* of 1914 as the 'Gay Bohemia' was between Redbourne and Princes Avenues. Entrance was through a long corridor (*ill. 39*) with summer gardens on one side and winter gardens on the other. The main hall could be used for dances as well as exhibiting films as the seats were removable. During the First World War it was used as a balloon factory (*ill. 38*) and later became a Kiwi blacking factory. Pulled down in the 1990s, it was replaced by a small housing estate. The iron gates in Ballards Lane are all that remain.

The Old Bohemia was succeeded by the New Bohemia, built on the site of a house called The

36. An election special at the Wentworth Hall in 1910.

WENTWORTH HALL

KINEMATOGRAPH.

Ballards Lane, Church End.

ON MONDAY, JANUARY 17,

AND FOR THREE DAYS ONLY,

Special

Election Picture:

" Scroggins Puts Up For Blankshire,

Or the Trials and Troubles of an Election Candidate."

PRICES AS USUAL.

37. *(left) A car sale room now in the old Wentworth Hall, Finchley's first cinema.*

38. *(below) The seats in the Old Bohemia in Ballards Lane were removed in 1917 to turn the building over to balloon manufacture.*

39. *(above) The entrance to the Old Bohemia cinema was the alley between Sony and Norwood.*

40. *The Old Bohemia cinema in its heyday.*

41. *The Arcadia Glider Skating Rink at Church End, which used rubber tyred skates.*

Limes, home of Hugh Taylor JP. Immediately south was the Arcadia Roller skating rink – part of its site is now occupied by Arcadia Avenue, off Regent's Park Road, and the rest by Gateway House.

VICTORIA PARK

Victoria Park was laid out on a large field on Cobley's Farm in 1902. In November 1914 a miniature rifle range was constructed to help train recruits before their service on the Western Front. This became a bowling green after the war. In the past few years the park has been the starting point for a much reduced Finchley Carnival.

43. Modern play facilities at the Victoria Park today.

42. The Finchley Carnival in June 1907.

44. *The White Lion on the Great North Road c.1905, a traditional stopping place for carters.*

East Finchley

Settlement at East End probably grew up during the fourteenth century along the line of the late thirteenth-century road from Highgate to the north, now the Great North Road (A1000). Pavage (the right to impose a local tax to pay for paving) was granted to the citizens of Barnet for the road from St Albans to Finchley Wood in 1347, so it must have been in existence before that date. The southern part of the road was called Newgate Lane in 1395 possibly a reference to the Bishop's gate near today's junction with East End Road. Newgate is also shown on Roque's map of 1756.

Hay was as important to London's economy as petrol is today – it was the fuel for the transport system. Hay and grass were grown throughout our district and carried into London on large haycarts which would offload and pick up return loads of manure and soot which were spread on the fields as fertiliser. A traditional stopping place for these carts was the White Lion, at to-day's junction with Bishop's Avenue, which was once called the Fleur de Lys and, because of the soot, was nicknamed 'the Dirthouse'. The Georgian version of this pub was taken down in 1938 and rebuilt.

The Bald Faced Stag on the west side of the junction of the High Road and East End Road was in existence by the 1730s. Also known as the Jolly Blacksmith, it was rebuilt about 1880. The junction was known as Park Gate, although the actual gate to the Bishop's Park and the related toll gate were further south at the foot of the hill next to the White Lion.

East Finchley station was opened in 1867 by the Great Northern Railway (later to be merged into the London & North Eastern Railway). Because the principal fuel for heating and cooking was coal, extensive storage sidings were built for local coal merchants. This was fortunate because since 1962 these have been used as a car park for the station. The line ran from Moorgate in the City through Finsbury Park to East Finchley and on to Finchley Church End. The electric railway, now part of the Northern line, was extended from Highgate (now renamed Archway) to East Finchley. The first electric train ran on 29 June 1939 and extensions to High Barnet and Mill Hill opened on 14 April 1940 and 18 May 1941 respectively by electrifying the old GNR lines. Because of wartime restrictions the rebuilding of the whole station was not completed until December 1949. Steam trains continued to run from the City until 1956.

45. *The High Road at East Finchley in 1904/5 when tramways were being laid.*

46. *East Finchley station c.1905 on the Great Northern Railway.*

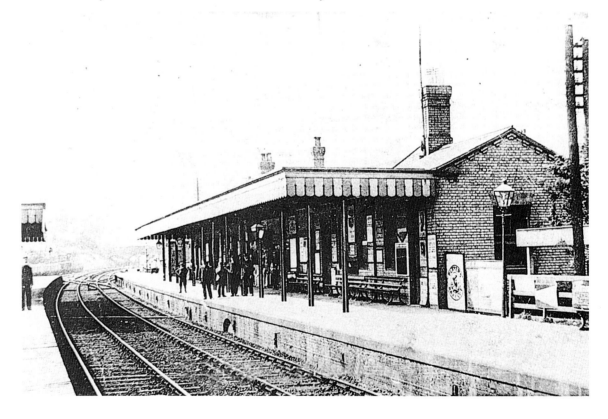

47. *Workers at Gray Brothers' coal yard at the East Finchley station sidings. This picture was taken in 1927.*

48. *The High Road at East Finchley c.1905 showing the railway bridge and the entrance to the coalyard of Gray Brothers.*

BISHOP'S AVENUE

Bishop's Avenue, originally running from Bishop's Wood to the Great North Road, was laid out about 1887 in large plots for expensive houses. By 1894 building had begun, mostly on single plots held on 99-year leases. William Dabbs, a builder from Stamford Hill took five acres in 1898 and the National Hospital for the Paralysed and the Insane took a plot near East Finchley station in 1895. But there were only about a dozen houses by 1906 and the nearby woods attracted tramps and rubbish dumping.

George Sainsbury, a scion of the Sainsbury grocery family, was living at Glenthorne in 1935 by which time the road was lined with houses on both sides. Another magnate was William Lyle, of the sugar refining business, who built East Weald in 1911.

Gracie Fields (1898-1979) lived at The Towers in Bishop's Avenue in the 1930s. She was awarded the Sylvaner Television Award in 1956 for Outstanding Entertainment Performances – in her case the capital letters are justified. Her strength was her versatility. She could dance, sing, act and do impersonations. She was trained during her early years in music hall and that, coupled with her great natural talent, exceptional singing voice and capacity for sheer hard work took her to the top. In 1938 she signed a Hollywood contract that made her the highest paid film star in the world, but unfortunately she contracted cancer in 1939. She is best remembered for her film and song *Sally in our Alley*, though she made over 500 records. She was made a DBE in 1979.

THE CINEMAS

The East Finchley Picturedrome is dated 1910 but opened in March 1912 in the High Road showing "The world's finest picture plays". Later called Coliseum, and later still the Rex Cinema, it is the oldest working cinema in the district and possibly in London. It was built by the Premier Electric Theatre Company on a plot of land made available by demolishing two large houses, Fairlawn and Cranleigh, both of which had entrances on Fortis Green Road. The builder was J.D. Pitcher of 251 Goswell Road in Clerkenwell.

It was refurbished and reopened as the Coliseum on 25 Jan 1926 with "a brilliant orchestra under the direction of Mr Lou Stevens, solo violinist". An extra entrance in Fairlawn Avenue was opened for the convenience of patrons using the back seats. During the winter of 1940-41 the Rex organised films for late workers by staying open until 10.00pm and 8.00pm on Sundays.

49. A car emerging from the Bishop's Avenue in 1935. To the left is the estate office for the Hampstead Garden Suburb, and a sign at the entrance to the avenue warns that it is a private road.

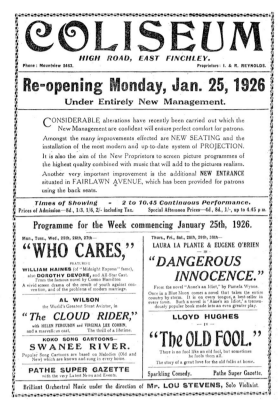

50. *A bill-of-fare at the reopening of the Coliseum cinema at East Finchley in January, 1926.*

51. *By 1935 the cinema's name had been changed to the Rex. This advertisement is for a week in 1941.*

A short-lived cinema called the Athenaeum Cinematograph Theatre opened in May 1910 near the corner of Huntingdon Road, when the *Finchley Press* advertised a continuous programme of up-to-date drama, comedy and travel for 6d and 3d for adults and 3d and 2d for children. The cinema went out of business when the Picturedrome opened.

Another famous show-business personality with connections to East Finchley was Peter Sellers (1925-1980), who was born into a theatrical family which included both parents and eight uncles. After service in the RAF during the war, he got a job with Ralph Reader's *Gang Show* and worked briefly at the Windmill Theatre. He was snapped up by the BBC where his talent as a 'man of many voices' was particularly appropriate. His varied and brilliant film career included *The Lady Killers, I'm alright Jack, Dr. Strangelove, The Millionairess,* and a whole series about Inspector Clouseau. His most popular roles however were in the *Goon Show* on radio. He lived for a time in Oakleigh Park South in Whetstone and also near East

Finchley station in a small flat with his mother.

An old path connecting the exit from the Bishop's Park with East End Road was later called The Causeway. Another ancient pathway skirting the edge of Finchley Common survives as The Walks.

FINCHLEY CHARITIES AND THE POOR HOUSE

Compared with other districts, Finchley was well endowed with charities. Robert Warren of Finchley left land in 1488 for the use of the church with the residue going to the poor. There were many other bequests and the charity eventually became a rich and substantial landowner. Four parish almshouses were built on Pointalls Meadow (between Long Lane and Oak Lane by 1614. These were condemned in 1739 but rebuilt as six double cottages. There were 16 aged inhabitants in 1805, 13 in 1850 and 14 in 1886.

Paupers who were not lucky enough to gain a place in the almshouses were often given 'outdoor relief', that is they were paid a weekly sum of money while they stayed in their own home. This parish relief was paid for by a Poor Rate on all property in the parish. There was also relief in kind – for example, clothing for girls to go into service, medical expenses, bread, food and fuel. Recipients receiving parish relief were not allowed to beg and had to wear a pauper's badge.

There was a workhouse for four adults and four

children at Fallow Corner (near what is now the Finchley Memorial Hospital and Granville Road) in 1768. When the lease expired, the vestry took a 21-year lease on the Five Bells in East End Road. Two rooms for the sick were added in 1805 and a smaller house in Green Street was leased in 1808 for about 10 inmates. This accommodation remained in use until 1835 when Barnet Union Workhouse was opened.

At a vestry meeting held on 17 August 1768 the following expenses were approved:

In the workhouse – Margaret Watson, Ann Ballon and her 3 children, Smith and child, Elizabeth Tyler, Harris' 2 children and James Austin.

One months butcher's bill for the house	8s 2d
Plat's bill for milk	6s 7d
Newsham's wine & beer	9s 10d
Dr Stephen's salary	£3 3 0d
Chandler's bill	2 11 4d
Ann Pinnel for nursing 4 weeks	£1 1 0d
Mr Clewing's bill for Osborne's rent	£1 2 6d
Harris for goods	£1 8 10d
Relief extra and casuals	£3 1 10d
Pensioners	£5 3 9d
Baker's bill	£2 15 5d
Mr Jones's bill	£2 18 0d
Expenses of the vestry	2 6d

The outdoor relief was
Widow Holder allowed 1s per week
Widow Blunden 1s
Mawl allowed a pair of shoes for the child that wants most
Ballon allowed a pair of shoes for each of her children
Moro's girl allowed a pair of stockings, a petty coat and a shift

Other pensions

Ruffing	2s
Moses	2 6d
Bonner	1s
Mawl	1s 6d
Grubb	1 9d
Heath	1s
Harris	3s 6d
Foxon	3s
Rolfe	1s
Wheeler	1s
Holder	1s
Blundon	1s

52. The scene near the Hog Market in about 1910.

THE HOG MARKET

Market Place was the original centre of East Finchley. Finchley Hog Market was opened by Thomas Odell. He had previously owned the George pub in Totteridge Lane and when it closed about 1680 he moved to a site in East Finchley near the main road and just south of East End Road, where he opened a new pub also called the George. He had kept pigs at Whetstone and in Finchley opened what became one of the largest specialised markets in the kingdom. Animals were kept in a nearby pound, later marked as Pound Road, a turning off Park Road. The market helped to sustain quite a few local pubs. The War Office billeting return of 1756 shows the Three Horse Shoes with room for three soldiers and three horses, the Three Conies (1 + 1) and the Queen's Head (2 + 1), all at the Hog Market. Kelly's directory of 1892 names the George and the Windsor Castle in Market Place.

Prospect Place was built about 1825 between the Market and East End Road.

Two notable local businesses were Clark's Bakeries, which opened in The Walks about 1927 – the name was changed to Merry Millers by 1963. At its peak about 200 people worked there. The nearby Advance Cleaners and Laundry employed about 175 people.

DEVELOPMENT

This area was heavily bombed during the night of 15/16 November 1940 when a large bomb fell causing more serious damage and casualties than any other local bomb. Eleven people were killed in the raid. The Auxiliary Fire Station at Leaver & Hemblings garage in the High Road was put out of action and water and gas mains were ruptured with the result that the High Road became impassable. At least ten nearby roads were blocked by debris. The doors of the post office in Market Place were blown off and the manager of Phillips off-licence at 145 High Road declared that 91 bottles of wine and spirits were destroyed.

After the war the council took the opportunity to redevelop the whole area, building a mixture of tower blocks and low level houses, a community centre and a youth club. Holy Trinity School was relocated here in 1974.

The opening of East Finchley station in 1867 encouraged development on the east side of the High Road where Baronsmere, Park Hall and Ingram Roads were laid out. These linked up to the Fortis Green estate, laid out from 1870 onwards by W. Collins who lived at Fortismere in Muswell Hill. This area contains many of the most pleasant houses in Finchley though much

53. The Hog Market looking north about 1870. Note the wide skirt of the landlady of the George Inn.

54. *The Hog Market looking south. This picture complements the previous one. Most of the houses appear Georgian.*

55. *Redevelopment at Market Place after the bombing of the Second World War.*

of it actually lies just outside the official boundary.

The shops in the High Road and the adjoining streets like Huntingdon Road were gradually built by small developers after the Ecclesiastical Commissioners released land on 99-year leases in 1879. Kitchener Road commemorates the relief of Khartoum in 1898; by 1896 about half of the plots in Bedford Road (where no. 56 is dated 1888 and 93/95 dated 1901) and Hertford Road (Victoria Terrace is dated Jubilee year 1897) had been occupied. The popularity of the Queen is obvious from names like Queen's Terrace, Queen's Parade. A feature of the whole estate is the use of decorated porches and stained glass over the front doors.

Creighton Avenue was laid out about 1900 but not extensively developed until 1920-30. Creighton House is typical of a mid-1930s property.

The spiritual needs of the district were not neglected. East Finchley Baptist Church in Creighton Avenue was founded in 1908 and East Finchley Methodist Church on the corner of High Road and Park Road dates from 1896 while the Salvation Army Citadel in Hertford Road is a little later. The Methodist building in the High Road was later converted into what is now the

56. *'Good class houses' on the Summerlee estate in 1927, from £900 each.*

57. *East Finchley Roman Catholic church, a remarkable building made of concrete with a brick exterior skin.*

58. *Martin School, built as the North Road School.*

Finchley Youth Theatre. Holy Trinity church in Church Lane was built in 1846 together with the vicarage to designs by Anthony Salvin. The adjacent church hall is dated 1913 and by the end of the twentieth century was used as the UK headquarters and religious and cultural centre of the Shree Aden Depala Mitramandel group.

East Finchley Congregational Chapel had been founded in various buildings near the Hog Market about 1804 but a new chapel was eventually built on the corner of Hog Road near the market and East End Road in 1851. This was demolished in 1963 when a smaller replacement was built nearby.

St Mary's Roman Catholic Church had used buildings in the High Road which were damaged by bombing in 1940. A replacement was opened in 1953. It is one of the earliest buildings in Europe to use pre-stressed concrete for the structure, which is lined with yellow brick.

East Finchley Public Library in the High Road was opened in 1938 by the mayor Alderman Pike.

North Road Elementary School had been built by Finchley Council just opposite the junction with Church Lane in 1912. The total cost of buying the land, building the school, together with the Handicraft centre, Combined Domestic Subjects centre, Medical Inspection Room and teachers' rooms, with all services was £14,750 plus £1,250 for furniture and fittings. The first head teacher was paid a salary of £185. The Senior Department was upgraded to become a Central School on 1 April 1920, but this soon became overcrowded and the school was transferred to Woodhouse Road in 1922. The site then reverted to elementary school status and now houses Martin Primary School. Air raid shelters can still be seen at the side of the school playing field.

59. *The former East Finchley library. In the year 1957/8 the book stock of the old borough of Finchley reached one million.*

CEMETERIES

The rapid increase in London's population and the great cholera epidemics of the 1830s and 1848 completely filled London's churchyards, resulting in legislation to provide public cemeteries managed by local authorities. In particular in 1853, 87 acres of the former Horse Shoe Farm in East Finchley were sold to the parish of St Pancras for £17,500. It was estimated that the laying out of the grounds and the construction of the chapels would cost an additional £7,500. The architects were Barnett and Birch of Holborn and the first interment was on 1 August 1854. It was the first publicly-owned cemetery in London. St Pancras had more land than it thought it could use and sold 30 acres to the parish of St Mary Islington but what they found was that by the 1870s they needed more ground, particularly for non-consecrated burials. So, in 1877 a further 94 acres, costing £20,000, were added from the Strawberry Vale estate; this land too was divided between St Pancras and Islington. The two parishes paid rates to Finchley but it was said that the passage through the area of some 10,000 corpses a year caused serious health problems,

though there was a corresponding increase in trade for the Bald Faced Stag. Kelly's Directory of 1892 shows six monumental masons and one funeral gardener having shops in the nearby High Road.

The central feature of the cemetery is the Mond mausoleum of grey granite and stone in Ionic style, probably one of the finest classical buildings in any London cemetery. Mond was a German industrialist whose collection of early Italian paintings was given to the National Gallery. Others interred here include the pre-Raphaelite artist Ford Madox Ford, Henry Croft, the first 'Pearly King', and Sir Horace Regnart, the inspiration for the development of Maple's furniture store in Tottenham Court Road.

St Pancras Court in the High Road was built on land surplus to the cemetery in the 1980s.

60. *The consecration of the St Pancras and Islington cemeteries in 1854.*

62. *St Pancras Court on the High Road, East Finchley, built on surplus cemetery land.*

61. *Islington's burial chapel.*

SOME VILLAINS

It would be nice to think that Dick Turpin frequented Finchley Common, but there is no evidence for this. 'Dick Turpin's oak' stood at the corner of Oak Lane and the notorious Jack Sheppard (1702-24) was captured not far from the present east entrance to the cemeteries.

Accounts of highwaymen were published in newspapers like the *Gentleman's Magazine*.

On July 11th 1699 as Mr Robert Leader and his servant were travelling from London across the common, they were attacked by Tooll and some of his companions. He knocked Leader from his horse and brutally stamped on his face and stomach, until he begged for his life. They let him rise and as he turned to walk away Tooll shot him in the back so seriously that he died the next day. When arrested in Jermyn Street London, Tooll resisted, firing a shot at the police and then attempting to stab one of them with a short sword. Even in court he continued to be aggressive, saying that he was only sorry that he had not stabbed the policeman in the heart. He was executed, unrepentant to the last, on 2 February 1700 and afterwards his body was put in chains on Finchley Common.

On 30th September, 1732:

A man on horseback coming over Finchley Common yesterday seven night was attacked by two highwaymen who demanded his money; but he, having more courage than conduct, knocked one of them down, upon which the other fired his pistol at him. The man, putting up his hand to save his head, the bullet shattered it all to pieces, so that he was obliged to have it cut off a few hours after.

In 1777:

On Sunday afternoon two gentlemen in a post chaise were robbed of their watches and £7 by three footpads near the eighth mile stone [which still stands outside Sainsbury's in North Finchley] on Finchley Common. The robbers told them they would probably be attacked again before they got to town by some of their accomplices and bade them the password 'Washington'. Accordingly when two fellows stopped the coach at about half past seven near Fog Lane, the gentlemen, upon repeating the above password were allowed to proceed without molestation.

The bodies of executed criminals were often sent to hospitals for dissection. Sometimes they were dipped in tar to repel carrion birds and gibbeted. There was a gibbet almost opposite the Bald Faced Stag and another at North Finchley near the Tally Ho.

Highwaymen were not romantic robbers of the rich to give to the poor. They were the exact equivalent of today's muggers and yobs.

In January 1820 a party of workmen were felling timber at Coldfall Wood to the east of Finchley Common. They discovered under the stump of an old oak tree, within four feet of the surface, two large wooden chests, much decayed, in which were deposited several tin boxes containing pistols, flints, remnants of wearing apparel, a quantity of brass buttons and a few silver coins of George II. It is supposed that they were placed there for safety many years earlier by some highwaymen.

The following is from the Middlesex Sessions records for 19 January 1614:

True bill against Elizabeth Rutter, widow, for having practised at Finchley certain wicked detestable and devilish arts called witchcrafts, enchauntments, charmes and sorceries, upon and against a certain Priscilla Fielde, daughter of James Fielde, so that the said Priscilla Fielde languished from 17 to 18 January, on which last day she died of the same arts being in this way murdered.
    Elizabeth Rutter was found guilty, sentenced and hanged.

It is worth noting the speed with which she was tried.

One of the purposes of enclosing the common was to reduce crime. In 1803 Sir John Sinclair, President of the Board of Agriculture said, "Let us not be satisfied with the liberation of Egypt or the subjugation of Malta, let us subdue Finchley Common". Sir Gilbert Elliott wrote explaining his late arrival for a meeting of the Board, "I shall not trust my throat on Finchley Common after dark".

63. F.R. Simms driving an early Daimler with a tricycle in the background.

SIMMS MOTORS

Plans for the development of the Red Lion estate, west of the High Road, for 18 blocks of flats were passed by Finchley Council in 1937. Oak Lane Health Centre was opened at the same time. The name Red Lion Hill first occurs in 1821, though as late as 1890 the district was sometimes called 'Cuckold's Haven'.

Nearby, on former common land between Long Lane and the Great North Road, was Simms motor units factory. F.R. Simms (1863-1944) was one of the cleverest men in a profession full of clever people. He was born in Germany where, when he was 28, he saw a light tramway in Bremen powered by a Daimler petrol engine. He obtained the rights to make Daimler cars in England and was also agent for De Dion, makers of high quality axles.

Simms was a skilful publicist and formed the first British Motor Car Club. Indeed, it is said that he invented the word 'motor car' as an alternative to 'horseless carriage', and he was a founder member of both the Automobile and Aero Clubs. He was described as "straight dealing and loveable" and also as "well read and cultivated". He

64. The drawing office at Simms' motor works.

65. *Simms Gardens, on the site of the former factory.*

produced the first drawing for gear driven cars for Daimler, invented armour plated vehicles for Vickers and Maxim, designed the first powered lawn mower for Ransoms, Sims and Jeffries and one of the first tractor drawn ploughs.

In 1907 he decided to give it all up in favour of Simms Magnetos based on the Bosch design. In 1911 he built a factory on the site of a house called The Grange in the High Road, together with six acres, to make, in particular, horns, petrol gauges, lighting sets and magnetos. The factory gradually diversified and became a substantial

local employer (by 1977 some 1600 people). It later merged with CAV.

Because it was so large Simms' factory induced a lively social activity including a football team and the firm's dances were renowned. During the war it had its own Home Guard unit and was on the Home Office list of sites to have priority for repair in the event of bomb damage. The factory was demolished and replaced by housing in 1991 and is remembered in Simms Gardens and Lucas Gardens.

MORE ALMSHOUSES

Pointalls was the name of eight acres of fields belonging to the Finchley Charities, at one time farmed by the Hayne family. Almshouses were built on the land near the High Road by 1776 and in 1958 new almshouses were erected with accommodation for a resident steward. In 1966 a further block was opened and named Wilmot Close after a former Finchley councillor. Yet more flats followed in 1972/3 (opened by Margaret Thatcher) and 1984. Thackrah Close is named after the father and son who were trustees of the charity for 55 years. There are now 102 almshouses.

In nearby Sylvester Road, four-bedroom houses were being offered for sale in 1907 for £330 each.

66. *Almshouses in Wilmot Close, opened in 1966 and named for a Finchley councillor.*

67. The entrance to the Strawberry Vale estate in the 1860s.

STRAWBERRY VALE

Finchley Common remained undeveloped except for a small settlement called Brownswell, mentioned by Norden in 1594, where the Great North Road crossed the Strawberry Brook. Strawberry Vale was bought, in 1816, by James Frost, a builder and farmer. He was a pioneer in the use of concrete for building houses and is said to have demonstrated the fire proof quality of the building by setting light to one room and holding a dinner party in the next room. Most of the farm buildings were demolished when the Strawberry Vale housing estate was formed in the 1970s.

The Green Man pub is shown in the War Office billeting return of 1756 as having rooms for three soldiers and stables for three horses. It was demolished and rebuilt in 1935, but finally destroyed when the North Circular Road was widened in 1993.

LONG LANE

Long Lane, possibly the medieval Ferrours Lane, is marked on the earliest maps and is named as such in 1719. The eastern section was called Broad Lane in 1814. Most of the houses are Victorian.

The fire station at the junction of Long Lane and the North Circular Road was built in 1936 together with a mortuary at the rear.

The first school in the district was the East End British School in Chapel Street in 1842 (enlarged in 1850). It was damaged by fire in 1860 and taken over by the local authority. By 1884, when it closed, it had about 180 children on the roll.

East Finchley Board School opened in Long Lane in 1884 with accommodation for 500 boys and girls (leaving at the age of 12) and for 250 infants. The school was renamed Alder School in 1931, became a secondary modern in 1944 and an all-boys' school in 1956. At the time of its closure in 1976 there were about 356 on the roll. It was replaced by Brooklands School and its site is now taken by Claybrook Close.

68. *Long Lane c.1905.*

69. *The East Finchley Board school in Long Lane, opened in 1884. It was renamed Alder School in 1931.*

The East End Road

East End Road is an ancient route connecting East End and Church End (central Finchley). The former Congregational Chapel (1878) on the corner of the High Road and East End Road has been replaced by a supermarket. A little further along was Holy Trinity School (1847), originally built as an Industrial school, that is one intended to teach the children a trade. The present building was later used to help children with limited mobility.

THE FIVE BELLS

In 1506 Thomas Sanny left three tenements and land called Foreryders, Stukefields and Manypenyes to the Finchley Charities. Confusingly this land was later called Homefield and Poor Tom's, though no reason for the change has been found. One of the properties on this land was a public house called the Five Bells. In 1484 Thomas Sanny, its owner, was fined four pence because "he was commonly accustomed to put 'lez hoppes' in the ale to the great damage and peril of the lieges of the king." At that time the property was described as two cottages with one brick chimney. A new Five Bells, essentially a beer-house, was built to the north-west of the old one, described in the War Office billeting return of 1756 as having room for one soldier, but with no stables. This building caught fire and was rebuilt in its present form in 1868. In the nineteenth century the Five Bells was often a training venue for bare-fist boxers. Matches, as well as races, took place on land (given to the parish in 1816 by Thomas Allen) in front of the pub.

Tony Gee in his meticulously researched book *Up to Scratch* quotes from newspaper accounts of those days.

> "Tom the Greek, for instance, fought Jack Carter on 20 May 1842 in a contest which Tom won after 76 rounds lasting 120 minutes. On 18 July 1843, George Sinclair, who had trained at the Five Bells, fought Ned Adams over 40 rounds lasting 203 minutes. The fight was declared a draw when both men were unable to continue. Tass Parker fought William Perry on 27 February 1844, and won after 133 rounds lasting 152 minutes, when Parker collapsed from exhaustion."

70. The Five Bells in East End Road, c.1905.

THE PLOWMAN FIRM

Nearby was a group of old cottages which were used as the parish Poor House. By 1811 they were in such a state of disrepair that they were demolished and replaced by three brick cottages each containing three rooms. Homefield House and Homefield Cottages were built about 1830 by James Plowman, member of a firm of local builders which survived for over 150 years. Part of the site was let in 1914 to the Finchley Presbyterian Lawn Tennis Club and has been used as a sports ground ever since. Homefield Cottages, nos 177 to 181 East End Road, were demolished in 1964.

Plowman and Co. may have been founded by Charles Plowman who is shown as a carpenter with premises in Ballards Lane before 1790. About 1825 Mark Plowman had a building firm in East Finchley and it was he who worked with Anthony Salvin on local buildings including the church and the school. The 1851 census shows him employing 15 men and 3 boys and making yellow stock bricks as well as operating as a builder.

Thomas Plowman lived near the Hog Market and employed 8 men on a brickfield in 1851. In 1873 Charles Plowman helped restore St Mary's church. The 1881 census shows him aged 48 living in Fir Cottage in Ballards Lane and employing 26 men and 2 boys in his building business and 10 men making bricks. He was also an energetic local politician. After his death in 1906 the firm abandoned brick making and the joinery business was eventually taken over by David Gomm who retained the old name and built a timber mill which was used for making school furniture. The mill closed about 1975.

SALVIN AND SANGER

Deansway and the rest of the Abbotts Gardens estate south of East End Road, dating from the early 1930s, exemplify the English obsession with building country dwellings in London suburbia featuring mock Tudor timber framing on the garages and highly elaborate window frames. Several large Victorian houses were built along East End Road, some of which were used as convents. Knightons was bought for the Poor Sisters of Nazareth in 1921 and East End House by the Sisters of the Good Shepherd in 1864. After 1972 this site, opposite St Marylebone Cemetery, was redeveloped for housing and for Bishop Douglass Secondary School and for Thomas More Way.

71. Elmshurst in East End Road, the home of architect Anthony Salvin.

Church Lane, connecting East End Road to the High Road, dates from about 1845 and is named from Salvin's Holy Trinity church – he also designed the vicarage. A road following a similar route is shown on Roque's map of 1756.

Anthony Salvin (1799-1881) was a leading authority on medieval architecture and his commissions included restoration work on Windsor, Alnwick and Carisbrooke castles. He designed numerous large country houses in the then fashionable mock Gothic style. Other buildings included three churches in Tynemouth and schools in Finchley, Highgate and Portsmouth. Perhaps his most romantic assignments were at Lanercrost and Holy Island in Northumberland.

The Salvin family actually lived from 1833 until 1857 in Elmshurst, a large house nearby on the south side of East End Road, possibly built in the late 16th century but with later alterations. This was demolished in 1939.

His church here gave its name to Trinity Road and Avenue and his house is remembered in Elmshurst Crescent to the south of East End Road, which dates from the 1970s and has a mixture of 2/3 storey flats and town houses with integral garages.

Just east of St Marylebone Cemetery, the former Park Farm (demolished 1959) occupied what is now Denison Close, Park Farm Close and Neale Close. An additional hundred acres of the farm were sold to build part of Hampstead Garden Suburb.

'Lord' George Sanger (1825-1911), who lived at Park Farm during his later years, was a leading circus proprietor. He was the first to use naphtha lighting to illuminate his conjuring act in 1848 and came to put on lavish shows at Astley's Amphitheatre in Westminster Bridge Road and at the Agricultural Halls in Islington. In 1886 his show 'The fall of Khartoum and the death of General Gordon', was advertised as involving 330 guards, 400 other supernumeraries, 100 camels, 200 real Arab horses, the fifes and drums of the Grenadier Guards and the fifes of the Scots Guards. This was followed by 'Gulliver's Travels', said to have been even more spectacular. He took his travelling circus to Paris for eleven years running and also to Balmoral and Windsor. With so many animals to keep and feed, he rented fields throughout the district. He was murdered by one of his own employees who then committed suicide.

ST MARYLEBONE CEMETERY

In common with the parishes of St Pancras and Islington (*see p46*), St Marylebone was also in need of cemetery space as its own parish filled with houses. In 1855 it opened a cemetery on some 33 acres of former farm land, designed (as was that of St Pancras) by Barnett and Birch. Those interred here include Sir George Barham, founder of Express Dairy (*see p24*), Austen Chamberlain, politician, Sir Edmund Gosse, man of letters, Quintin Hogg, founder of the Regent Street

73. Memorial to Sir Peter Nicoll-Burnett (1816-1905). A splendid example of Victorian funereal art.

72. A balcony in Trinity Road.

74. *The consecration of St Marylebone Cemetery in March 1855.*

Polytechnic, Thomas Huxley, Leopold Stokowski, conductor, and Jimmy Nervo, member of the Crazy Gang.

MANOR FARM

The old Manor Cottage Tavern stood by the route of the later North Circular Road. It was rebuilt in 1934 when the road came through, but demolished completely when it was widened. Manor Farm stood roughly between Finchley Cricket Club's ground on the northern side of the North Circular and the Tavern. It too was used by Sanger's circus largely to provide fodder but also as winter quarters for animals.

From 1879 until 1897 the farm was occupied by wealthy store owner William Whiteley (1831-1907). He was inspired by a visit to the Great Exhibition of 1851 to start a small business at 31 Westbourne Terrace in Bayswater employing two female assistants. His revolutionary ideas included attractive window displays with clear price

tickets and delivery anywhere in the country by post. He eventually owned a conglomeration of 21 shops in the vicinity selling fancy drapery, food, drink and furniture and by 1899 he was said to be worth over a million pounds. As with George Sanger, Whiteley's death was also a sensation, for he was shot in his vast shop by a deranged man who claimed to be his illegitimate son.

About 1911, 68 acres of Manor Farm were sold for building development to become Briarfield and Rosemary Avenues. A back room at no. 4 Rosemary Avenue was fortified in 1940 to provide protection for a machine gun to cover the railway bridge in Squires Lane.

DEARD'S

In 1912 more land was purchased by Robert Deard, who ran an enormous haulage business based in Camden Town, providing horses for towing canal barges. He also used horses and carts and lorries for local deliveries. He died aged 65 in 1931. As

75. *Manor Cottage Tavern in East End Road, before the building of the North Circular.*

76. *Deard's Finchley Carnival float in the 1970s.*

the business was underfinanced, it was formed into a limited company which obtained contracts to clear night rubbish from various markets and to clear household refuse from St Pancras (1933) and Finchley (1935). This business expanded to such an extent that virtually all north London's domestic refuse from St Pancras northwards to Bushey and Potters Bar was transported by Deard's to infill sites at Cole Green in Hertfordshire. By 1953 the Manor Farm site was in the middle of a residential area and Deard's was relocated to a site at the junction of the North Circular Road and Colney Hatch Lane. The business has diversified since then and by the end of the century the main focus was on property.

Their old site is now used by the Middlesex Cricket Club Indoor School and a fitness centre.

SQUIRES LANE

Squires Lane, originally Place Lane, joins East End Road to Long Lane and the High Road. Claigmar Vineyard, on its north-west just by the railway, on either side of Oakfield Road, is remembered today in Claigmar Gardens. In 1899 it had about 18° acres under glass and was said to produce 100 tons each of tomatoes and grapes and over a quarter of a million cucumbers. The former fishpond belonging to the Manor House and mistakenly called a moat, was filled in about 1907. This lay between Briarfield Avenue and East End Road.

The section of road eastwards from Long Lane was called Short Lane. It is almost entirely late Victorian and Edwardian, as are the roads running from it. There were brick fields near the junction with Long Lane which of course were used during development.

The Finchley Corporation Electricity Works in Squires Lane were opened in 1903 originally supplying about 130 houses with direct current. Street lights were added and the supply was gradually extended, being converted to alternating current about 1936. In an attempt to persuade customers to use electricity rather than gas, Finchley Council had a scheme whereby an electric cooker, complete with all utensils, was supplied free of charge It was in the mid thirties too that gas street lights were replaced by electric lamps. The water to cool the machines used in the works was drawn from a deep well specially dug and stored in two large ponds which, because it was warm, proved attractive to mosqui-

77. Squire's Lane c.1905 looking south with the Manor House in the distance.

78. *The Finchley Electricity Works in Squires Lane.*

tos. Goldfish were put into the ponds to control the mosquitos to such good effect that some fish grew to more than a foot long. The Works had its own Home Guard unit in the 1939 war.

The public slipper and swimming baths further down Squires Lane, opened in 1915, provided not just a pool for entertainment, but facilities for private baths at a time when many people had to rely on a tin bath on the floor of the kitchen. There were also provisions for families to do their clothes washing – an early example of what became launderettes. The swimming bath was 165 feet long by 50 feet wide with a depth varying from 3ft 6in to 7 feet and held about 270,000 gallons. It was proposed to run water from the deep well at the Squires Lane Electricity Works, which would be warmed by passing through the cooling plant. It was felt that running the water through the bath would keep it clean and reduce the expense of changing the water so frequently, but the scheme was not a success and conventional coke fired boilers were fitted instead. The baths were demolished in 2000 and replaced by Douglass Court. Behind the site of the pools the allotments cover part of the old Finchley Common.

Manorside School, originally called Squires Lane School, was an all age school opened in 1903 with 410 pupils and eight teachers. It became a girls' school in 1956 and is currently used for primary pupils. By 2001 there were about 265 children organised into 10 classes.

Squires Lane runs east to the High Road and was built up steadily in the Edwardian period. Finchley Urban District Council built 60 cottages in Squires Lane in 1902 and the remainder of the district is made up of terraced private houses.

Tudor Junior and Infant School was built in Queens Road in 1952 and a Nursery was added in 1975. It has accommodation for about 300 pupils in all.

Two newspaper adverts relating to the area from the 1880s are worth recording:

Wanted by a LADY – a good plain cook. Cow and other staff kept.

Wanted – a family's washing in Long Lane. Own grass. [Laying washing flat on the grass enabled the sun to bleach the whites.]

Finchley Manor House

Finchley was called a manor as early as 1374, over which the Bishop of London claimed rights "since time out of mind". It may have been included in the 50 hides of land which Tyrhtel, Bishop of Hereford, granted to Wealdheri, Bishop of London, about 704. Finchley was treated as part of Fulham until it was transferred to the Lordship of Hornsey in 1491.

The present Manor House in East End Road opposite Squires Lane is described by Pevsner as "a good square house of the early nineteenth century with a Doric porch", though it was actually built for Thomas Allen about 1723. It stands on the site of a much earlier settlement.

In 1504 there was a house here "within the moat". This is possibly the moat at the rear of the house examined by HADAS in 1990 with inconclusive results.

The site was originally probably part of the de Basing estate. Adam de Basing was chief minister and "well beloved friend" to King Henry III. He bought land in 1253 for 300 marks and more in 1257 and 1260, using it for sheep farming – the names 'Mutton Brook' and 'Sheep House Farm' are reminders of this. He died in 1262.

In 1662 Edward Allen bought the manor for £5,000. He was a fishmonger, but sufficiently wealthy to be an Alderman of the City of London in 1620 and Sheriff of London in 1621. In his will he left "to the Poore of ffinchley – tenne pounds to be distributed at the discrecion of my wife to the poore inhabiting neere Eastend there".

Sir Thomas Allen married Mary Weld in 1627. They had seven daughters and six sons, all of

79. Finchley Manor House and, inset, the so-called Turpin's Oak (see p48).

whom were baptised at St Mary's church. He was an MP and Deputy Lord Lieutenant of Middlesex and was a prominent patron of the Finchley Charities. The estate remained with the Allen family for some 200 years before passing to Edward Philip Cooper (a distant relative), who received "The Manor of Finchley with appurtenances and six messuages, twelve barns, twelve stables, ten dovehouses, ten gardens, 300 acres of land, 80 acres of waste land, 250 acres of meadow, 200 acres of pasture and common of pasture and turbary".

The manor house was used for a private school from 1838 until 1862, when George Plunknett moved in. He was a local magistrate and used to hold court in his house. In 1882, "by direction of the owner George Plunknett Esq., J.P. removing, the house is offered for sale by auction". At about the same time much of the surrounding land was sold for housing, partly by Edward Arden, after whom Arden Road is named. By 1905 A.W. Gamage, head of the large store in Holborn, lived at the house which, in 1915, was requisitioned and used for the recuperation of wounded soldiers.

Albert Gamage (1855-1936) founded his shop in Holborn in 1878 and amalgamated it with Bentick & Co. in 1908. The business was widened in scope to include all kinds of leisure activities, such as gardening, camping and motor supplies, and was as famous for its good value as for the maze of showrooms which made up his store. He was a keen supporter of Finchley charities, especially of working men's clubs. Gamage sold the house in 1918 to the Sisters of the Society of Marie Auxiliatrice, who used it both as a convent and as a school.

The manor house is now occupied by the Sternberg Centre. The immense contribution to the intellectual, cultural and scientific life of this country made by the Jewish community is out of all proportion to the very small number of Jewish people who live here.

The Sternberg Centre is Europe's largest Jewish cultural centre, named after one of its major benefactors, Sir Sigmund Sternberg. It is the base of the Reform Synagogues of Great Britain, and they conduct services in both Hebrew and English. Families sit together, and both men and women may lead services and serve as rabbis.

The Centre manages the Akiva Primary School – the first Jewish primary school to be built under the auspices of the progessive Jewish movement – and also the Leo Baeck College, Europe's only seminary for the training of progressive rabbis. In the rear gardens at the centre is the Holocaust Memorial, a simple black monolith, inscribed with the word 'Zachor', meaning 'remember'.

80. Prince Philip with children at the Akiva Primary School in 1996.

The North Circular

The maximum speed for motor cars had been extended to 20 mph in 1903 and by then it was clear that cars were here to stay. In 1914 and 1915 there was a series of conferences at the Local Government Board in Whitehall to plan a number of arterial roads. These included the North Circular Road to run from the new Great West Road near Gunnersbury through Willesden and on to Edmonton. After the First World War, road construction was given a high priority and under the Unemployment (Relief Works) Act of 1920 stretches of land were purchased. The North Circular was planned to be 100 feet wide, made up of three lanes. Work on the Willesden section began in 1921. Progress on the Hendon/Finchley section as far as the Great North Road at Brownswell was relatively easy. Strawberry Brook and Dollis Brook were both put into culverts, but there was a real problem in constructing a new tunnel at New Southgate under the main railway line to Scotland, and in 1926 the New Southgate section is shown on the maps as "planned". There was also a new road connecting Henley's Corner with the A41 at Mill Hill that was later to form part of the Barnet by-pass. Subsequent improvements have included the creation (in the 1980s) of underpasses at Finchley and at Friern Barnet Lane and large scale works at Henley's Corner.

LA DELIVRANCE

La Delivrance (locally called 'Dirty Gertie') is the name of the large bronze statue of a naked woman standing at the junction of the North Circular Road and Regent's Park Road. It was presented to the citizens of Finchley by Viscount Rothermere and unveiled on 20 October 1927 by Lloyd George. The figure stands fifteen feet high to the tip of the sword and is the work of the French sculptor Guillaume. It was inspired by the Allied victory over the Germans at the Battle of the Marne fought between 15 and 19 July 1918.

Lord Rothermere said that he had known Finchley all his life and that he had lost count of the number of times that he and his brother Lord Northcliffe had passed through the district on their way to visit their mother at Totteridge.

Lloyd George said that we must never forget the meaning of the word 'Delivrance'. We are apt to forget, he said, "the ruin of war, the wreckage of war, depression and reaction that follows war and the burdens of war. Europe had been subjected to one resistanceless military tyranny, that is what we had escaped from. The great task for humanity is not escape by the sword, it is escape from the sword. We must never forget that this was the war to end all war!"

The statue was dedicated by the Revd Stewart Bernays, Rector of Finchley.

81. The junction of the North Circular Road and Falloden Way in 1933.

82. The unveiling of La Delivrance by Lloyd George in 1927.

THE BARNET BY-PASS

Aylmer Road, (named after a former Bishop of London) Lyttelton Road and Falloden Way formed part of the Barnet by-pass planned in the 1920s. The roads skirted the northern edge of the Hampstead Garden Suburb, where leases were granted from 1909. Some houses were built to the designs of G.L. Sutcliffe and C.G. Butler. Sutcliffe (1863-1915) was appointed architect to the Co-partnership Tenants, a non-profit making company which had built houses at Brentham in Ealing as well as at Hampstead. He designed Meadway Court and a close is named after him in Hampstead.

The boundary of the Bishop's park ran across Lyttelton Road playing fields, where part of the hedge dating from the thirteenth century is still visible.

Ribbon development began almost immediately and there were houses all along the north side by 1933. There was also in-filling on the Stanhope Avenue, Mountfield Road, Windermere Avenue estate running north to East End Road at the same time.

An ancient track known as Ducksetters Lane ran from Hampstead via Temple Fortune, across the River Brent or Mutton Brook and up Gravel Hill to Church End. In 1827 a new turnpike road from Marylebone to Tally Ho Corner was opened with one of the tollgates at the junction with East End Road. The southern end locally was called Regent's Park Road and the northern end Ballards Lane.

The marshy nature of the district is shown by a field name like Rushy Field, now covered by the North Circular Road. The houses from Manor Parade to Beechwood Avenue are on Spring Field. This was the site of the Finchley Spa, popular in the eighteenth and nineteenth centuries and the water of which was said to be good for the eyes. The actual spa was near Arden Road and Ryefield, Mustard Field and Great Barn Field were nearby. There were watercress beds near Crest Gardens and Fairholme Close.

83. The Rough Lots, a remaining part of Finchley Common.

The Glebe Lands

Apart from Coldfall Woods, all that is left of the old Finchley Common is the Glebe Lands off the High Road opposite Squires Lane, but unfortunately the site has been vandalised and neglected for over fifty years. Known locally as the 'Rough Lots', it was used in the nineteenth century to supply gravel for the Great North Road. There is an attractive nature trail with informative notice boards running through what is left.

Glebe land originally was that assigned to the Incumbent of a parish as part of his benefice, and it was often worked on free of charge by parishioners.

Finchley Drill Hall at 444 High Road was opened in 1937 at a time when there was an expansion of the Territorial Army, with a particular emphasis on recruiting for anti-aircraft defence. Recruitment locally was to the 171 (Finchley) Battery of the 61st Anti-Aircraft Brigade, which had converted from a rifle unit in 1936. By July 1937 about 350 officers and men and 72 cadets were involved. They were equipped with 3.7 inch A.A.

guns, one of the finest weapons of the Second World War. It fired a shell weighing about 28 lbs to a height of 32,000 feet. On Friday 13 June 1937 they made history by becoming the first Territorial Army anti-aircraft unit ever actually to hit its target – a Queen Bee radio controlled aircraft flying straight and level at 3,800 feet at 100mph.

The Battery was posted to its initial war station at Orsett in Essex in September 1939 as part of the ring of A.A. defences around London. In October 1941 the battery was at Woodford and in 1942 at Genoch, a training camp in South Wales. In 1943 the unit was sent to the Middle East where it remained until the end of the war.

After the war the drill hall reverted to Territorial Army status and by 1950 was used by 490 AA (TA) Battery. In 1999, 3 Company of the 10th Battalion the Parachute Regiment with its attached Assault Pioneer Platoon used the hall.

In 1916 a 3-inch anti-aircraft gun had been placed just behind the Drill Hall. The site was covered by tennis courts in the 1930s, though it was still referred to as Finchley Gun Site.

84. A very crowded scene at Finchley swimming pool. Sometimes the overcrowding would lead to a rationing system of use.

THE SWIMMING POOL

Finchley's open air swimming pool was the Council's pride and joy. Opened in 1932, it had an imposing entrance with a restaurant and viewing platform. There were two pools, one for children and a nine-foot deep adult pool with two diving boards. There was a large grassed sun-bathing and picnic area and in summer months the pools were so popular that a rationing system was introduced involving coloured bands. At times the loud speakers would announce "All bathers with blue bands to leave the water please". On August Bank Holiday Monday 1937 over 4,000 bathers used the pools on a day when temperatures soared to the eighties.

This lovely pool has now gone and is replaced by a large leisure complex.

The land further north was used for sports pitches and by Finchley Football Club from 1930. The team had originally played at a ground in Long Lane and had used the Railway Hotel at Church End for its meetings. Perhaps the best known player was George Robb who also played for Spurs. The team is now called Wingate.

Bow Lane, veering west off the High Road, is shown on the 1754 map and is so called because of its shape. It was built up around 1900 and ran

85. The opening ceremony of the children's pool at Finchley in July 1934.

BOROUGH OF FINCHLEY

Opening of the Children's Open Air Bathing Pool

GREAT NORTH ROAD, N.12

By The Right Honourable The Lord Mayor of London

THURSDAY, 12th JULY, 1934

Order of Proceedings

AT THE BOROUGH BOUNDARY

(Regents Park Road).

4 p.m.

ARRIVAL OF :

THE RIGHT HONOURABLE THE LORD MAYOR OF LONDON
(Sir Charles Henry Collett) accompanied by
The Lady Mayoress (Lady Collett),
Alderman and Sheriff Sir George Broadbridge and Lady Broadbridge,
Colonel and Sheriff S. G. Joseph and Mrs. Joseph.

THE LORD MAYOR will be received by His Worship the Mayor of Finchley (Councillor Vyvyan Wells) accompanied by the Town Clerk (Mr. H. Wood Barter), after which he will proceed to the Children's Bathing Pool, Great North Road, via Tally Ho ! Corner.

AT THE CHILDREN'S BATHING POOL

GUARD OF HONOUR will be formed by a detachment of "A" Company, 1st Cadet Battalion, Middlesex Regiment, Christ's College Cadet Corps.

PROGRAMME OF MUSIC by the Band of the 56th (First London) Divisional Engineers (T.A.).

86. The modern Finchley leisure centre.

87. Finchley County School.

to Fallow Corner. Our Lady of Lourdes Catholic School was opened here in 1929, with extensions in 1956. The older pupils moved to Bishop Douglass School in 1963. A purpose-built nursery was due to open in September 2001 and, excluding this, there are now about 230 pupils on roll.

Finchley County School was built on the Great North Road in 1903 to provide full time education for pupils aged up to 16. It was taken over by Middlesex County Council in 1909 and by the 1930s it had a distinguished academic record. However, the location was too small to house a comprehensive school and in 1971 the pupils were transferred to Manorhill School and the site became the borough's professional development centre.

Fallow or Cobley's Farm ran from Ballards Lane to the High Road and to Squires Lane in the south. It was probably in existence by 1429. The exact extent of the early buildings is unclear.

The three 'Ends' of Finchley, Church End, East End and North End met at Fallow Corner, at roughly the junction of the Great North Road, Summers Lane and Granville Road. Charles Dickens stayed at the farm briefly while writing part of *Martin Chuzzlewit*, a fact commemorated by Dickens Avenue off Squires Lane. The farm was occupied by the Cobley family from 1680 for about 200 years – it was demolished about 1900. it extended from Ballards Lane to the High Road and to Squires Lane in the south. Owned by the Clulow family in 1822, but still let to the Cobleys, it was renamed Etchingham Park after the Clulow home in Sussex and was sold in 1880 for development. The old name of the farm survives in Fallow Court Avenue.

Joseph Grimaldi the great clown lived in Fallow Cottage in what is now Granville Road. He was born into a family of dancers and entertainers on 18 December 1779 and died on 31 May 1837. He made his stage debut at the age of two at Sadler's Wells Theatre and for a number of years he appeared simultaneously at two theatres, running from one to the other. In 1806 he appeared at Covent Garden in a new type of pantomime called *Harlequin and Mother Goose*. He played a new kind of clown, a combination of rogue and simpleton, criminal and innocent victim. His last performance was at Sadler's Wells in 1828. He was the most famous clown in English stage history and in recognition many of today's clowns are called Joey.

The Wright-Kingsford Home stood for many

88. Joe Grimaldi.

years in Granville Road. In September 1898 two hospital nurses, Miss Blanch Wright and Miss Ellen Kingsford, rented a cottage at Hersham in Surrey as 'a home for homeless babies'. In April 1902 they took on a large house in Granville Road to accommodate about forty children. The building was found to be insanitary, but with help from the Revd H.S. Miles £1,000 was raised and the premises purchased. Financial problems continued until Sir John Kirk, Chairman of the Shaftesbury Society took an interest and the future was secured. A feature was the annual fête organised by the Ladies' Entertainment Committee, which raised over £1,000 annually for many years. In 1937 Princess Mary opened a new £8,000 extension to increase provision to 100 children, who wore a distinctive red and blue uniform.

By 1945 the buildings had become dilapidated and were no longer fit for use by children. After a brief period as a nurses' home the buildings were demolished in the 1950s.

Nearby was Fallow Lodge, later Holdenhurst, where the Goodyear family lived. Alderman Frederick Goodyear died in 1937, though the house was demolished about 1905. Holdenhurst

89. *The Wright-Kingsford Home for orphans.*

90. *An unusual piece of modern design tucked away at 36 Granville Road.*

and Chislehurst Avenues now cover the site. About 1880 the land bordering Ballards Lane was let to Frederick Wheeler for housing development.

FINCHLEY MEMORIAL HOSPITAL

The earliest hospital in Finchley was in two rooms attached to the workhouse in 1805. Other than that, those who could afford it paid a doctor to attend, those who could not made the best of it or died.

Finchley Cottage Hospital was built in 1908 on a site near Fallow Corner given by Ebenezer Holman, who lived at Friern Watch in the High Road, north of Tally Ho Corner – his bust has since been stolen from the entrance foyer of the hospital. It was enlarged to 46 beds and renamed Finchley Memorial Hospital in 1922. A private wing was added in 1933 and by 1973 there were 127 beds.

During the Second World War this was a receiving hospital for Finchley and Friern Barnet and Sir Girling Ball of St Bartholomew's Hospital was appointed to oversee medical arrangements. The first admissions were on the night of 22 September 1940, when a boy of about nine was admitted with his left leg almost completely severed. The climax came on the night of 15 November 1940 when there was heavy bombing in the High Road, East Finchley and in Ossulton

91. Finchley Memorial Hospital c.1908.

Way. Twenty-seven casualties arrived by ambulance and some staff worked non-stop for fourteen hours.

The establishment of the Barnet Health Authority led to a rationalisation of facilities with a concentration on the Barnet site and by the end of the twentieth century most treatment at Finchley was for day patients. A geriatric unit with a garden attached was built in 1980.

The Finchley Carnival was originally established in the early 1900s to raise funds for the widows and children of soldiers in the Boer War, but the proceeds were later used for the hospital.

Summers Lane, on the other side of the High Road, was originally a footpath leading across Finchley Common to the north of Glebe Farm to Dunger Place and Halliwick Manor House in Friern Barnet. Large parts of the common were used for playing fields and allotments thereby preserving at least a lung of fresh air.

A large housing estate centred on Ingleway was planned by Finchley Council in 1915 and construction went on steadily from 1919.

Summerside School in Crossway was built in 1933 with places for 450 juniors and infants, but after 1939 a separate infant school was in use. There were further alterations in 1968 and 1973

92. The opening of the casualty wards at Finchley Memorial Hospital in February 1927.

FINCHLEY MEMORIAL HOSPITAL.

PUBLIC OPENING

— OF —

CASUALTY WARDS

— BY —

LADY BARRATT

— ON —

Thursday, 24th February, 1927,

at 3 o'clock.

A Dedication Service will be Conducted by

The Right Revd. The LORD BISHOP OF WILLESDEN.

93. Looking east at Ingleway in Summers Lane on 10 June 1921.

and by the end of the century there were about 350 pupils on the roll with about 30 teaching and non-teaching staff.

The Finchley Corporation Sewage Farm and Rubbish Disposal Yard were opened on 100 acres of land in 1885 on the south side of Summers Lane and running down to Strawberry brook. It remained in use until 1963. In 1889 an isolation hospital was built nearby, perhaps too near the sewage plant, but it remained in use until Coppetts Wood Hospital was opened in 1922. A mortuary was built nearby and used until the new fire station and mortuary were opened in 1935 (*see p51*). At first household waste was buried on the site in order to improve levels, and more was dumped under what are now the nearby playing fields. For many years the domestic rubbish was removed by Deard's (*see p56*), the contractors, to infill sites at Coles Green in Hertfordshire. Some rubbish still goes to infill and some to incineration at Picketts Lock, Edmonton.

The sewage farm grounds eventually became subsumed in the widened North Circular Road, in Tesco supermarket, the nearby garage and ambulance station. The brick works and kilns in Summers Lane shown on a map of 1895 are now used for housing in the form of Christchurch Close.

Manorhill School in Summers Lane was formed in 1971 by the amalgamation of Finchley County, Hillside and Manorside secondary schools. Renamed Compton School, it was the first purpose-built comprehensive school to be constructed by the new London Borough of Barnet and by the end of the century it had an annual budget of some two million pounds. It was named after Denis Compton, one of England's most successful and famous cricketers.

Compton (1918-1997) was an exuberant player of the game. His career batting average was 51.85 and his test match average scarcely lower at 50.06. He made his test match debut at Nottingham against the Australians at the age of 20 when he made 102. He scored 184 at Trent Bridge against Miller and Lindwall bowling very fast in poor light. At Old Trafford he sustained a cut eyebrow which needed stitches and returned heavily bandaged to make another century. He was no mean footballer either, winning a cup winner's medal with Arsenal in 1950, and he played golf with skill and enthusiasm.

Dunger Place, built soon after 1840 on common land at the east end of Summers Lane, was named after Henry Dunger who lived with his wife in the Triumph Public House in 1841 when he had two resident servants.

Friern Barnet

The place name Friern Barnet derives from the area's possession by the Knights of St John of Jerusalem, alternatively known as Knights' Hospitaller. Friern is a corruption of 'freren', the plural of 'frere', meaning brother, as the knights often referred to each other. Barnet, or 'bærnet', meant a place cleared by burning.

The Bishop of London, with the consent of the Dean and Chapter of St Paul's Cathedral, granted to the Knights "the land of Barnet which Picot the Lombard held", together with the church and wood. This grant was confirmed by King John in 1199, and the wording at that time suggests an early link between Friern Barnet and Finchley and Hornsey rather than with Barnet.

This part of our district was always sparsely populated. The hamlet of Colney Hatch, identified in the fifteenth century, was reckoned in 1795 to have only 12 of the 78 houses in the parish, and these were mostly large establishments of well-to-do families. The derivation of 'Colney' is obscure, but 'Hatch' almost certainly indicates a gate.

THE ORANGE TREE

The earlier route from London to the north of England, via Colney Hatch Lane met the east-west route (Woodhouse Road and Friern Barnet Road) to Betstyle near the old settlement of Halliwick. This was an attractive site, where a house used for parish meetings was licensed as an inn in 1596. It is said that Sir Walter Raleigh brought back an orange tree which he gave to his uncle, Sir William Carey, the owner of this house, who planted it in an orchard to the rear. Carey also owned what became Friary Park to the west of Friern Barnet Lane.

In 1558 Queen Elizabeth, on her way from Hatfield House to London for her coronation, took the route down Friern Barnet Lane. She stopped for refreshment at the well opposite the church, but finding this not to her liking went on to the Crown inn (the earlier name of the Orange Tree) where the vessel from which she drank sack was kept for many years. Norden tells us that Sir John Popham, Lord Chief Justice during the reign of Elizabeth, occasionally made his home at the manor house in Friern Barnet. Popham was buried in the church of St James's.

94. The Orange Tree in c.1900.

95. *The Priory in Friern Barnet Lane. This 200-year-old building was taken over by the Friern Barnet Urban District Council in 1906. It was pulled down in 1939 when the construction of the adjacent Town Hall began.*

About 1675 Charles II and Nell Gwyn were visitors to the Carey family in Friary Park, and it is about this time that the name Orange Tree is first used. In 1874 the pub was taken over by Septimus Emberson, who heard the tale of the orange tree and planted a replacement, which grew to a considerable size. In 1909 the Orange Tree was rebuilt in mock-Tudor style and the site of the orange tree was marked by a stone slab and was further commemorated by a row of cast-iron orange trees. The coat-of-arms of the Carey family was included in the pargeting on the front wall.

THE TOWN HALL

The Friern Barnet Local Board first met in 1884 in the St James's church school room. Later its offices were at 18 Beaconsfield Road until 1906, when they moved to The Priory, a 200-year old building at the junction of Friern Barnet Road and Lane opposite the Orange Tree. This was demolished in 1939 and replaced by the existing Town Hall designed by John Brown and Henson. The looming threat of war that year caused a change

in design to include an underground Civil Defence control centre. This and the shortage of labour and materials meant that the building was not fully functional until 1944. It is now used by the borough's education department.

In 1886 the Board's single employee combined the duties of a sanitary inspector, rate collector and road surveyor.

The comedian Cyril Fletcher, famous on the radio during and after the last war, was the son of a former town clerk of Friern Barnet and went to Woodhouse School. His talent for writing and performing was apparent at an early age. His 'Odd Odes', were as familiar as the sounds of sirens during the war, though his phrase "Pin back yer lug'oles, odd ode number one coming up", was a good deal less threatening. He also appeared in straight theatre and was a marvellous pantomime dame.

Next to the Town Hall was the fire station, opened in 1927. The first Friern Barnet Brigade, formed in 1907, had three hose cars, three hand escapes and three jumping sheets. The part-time firemen were summoned by cycle messengers, but in 1909 fire alarm bells were fitted in their

96. Friern Barnet Town Hall in 1945, celebrating the end of the war.

houses and Pompier ladders and belts were purchased. In 1926 a Dennis fire engine was bought and the brigade reorganised to include thirteen retained fire fighters.

The first electric traffic lights in the district were erected in Friern Barnet in January 1934 – they were described as "vehicular actuated traffic signals".

The estate called Southgate Park, on the north side of Friern Barnet Road included The Priory; this was developed piecemeal after the bankruptcy of its owners, the London Land Company in 1887. Stanford, Ramsden and Hartland Roads are now on its site.

Friern Barnet library, opened in 1934, was the first purpose-built library to be erected by the Middlesex County Council. It cost £3,782, of which £1,400 came from the Carnegie Trust. Before that, public library provision consisted of some cupboards of books at St James's school, St Peter's school and The Priory.

St John's church opened in a temporary corrugated iron building in 1883 on the north side of Friern Barnet Road, but its replacement was on the opposite side of the road on a site given by George Knights Smith. It was built between 1887 and 1891 to the designs of John L. Pearson who

97. The laying of the foundation stone for Friern Barnet Library on 23 September, 1933.

ORDER OF PROCEEDINGS

at the

LAYING OF THE FOUNDATION STONE

of the

Friern Barnet County Library

by

Mr. COUNTY COUNCILLOR C. H. BARBER

98. Friern Barnet Library, opened in 1934.

modelled it on a Rhineland chapel. Unfortunately many of its best features are not visible from the road.

Hillside Farm occupied the land between Friern Barnet Road and Colney Hatch Lane, west of the church. This was developed as the Hollyfield estate *c.*1910.

A building next to the Orange Tree was the White House, which had an estate of 55 acres west of Friern Barnet Lane and north of Woodhouse Road. George Knights Smith occupied it until his death in 1886. Much of the estate was developed before the First World War with such roads as Ashurst, Petworth, Bramber, Buxted and Warnham.

The famous footballer, Alex James, lived at 24 Friern Barnet Lane. Born in Lanarkshire, 'Wee Alex' was probably England's best-known footballer of the day, famous for his baggy shorts. He made his debut for Arsenal against Leeds United on 31 August 1929 and usually functioned as a tactical mid-field player. After his retirement in 1937 he worked for a brief period as a journalist before returning to Highbury in 1945 as a coach. He died suddenly in June 1953, aged only 51.

THE BACON FAMILY

John Bacon leased "the manor of Whetstone in the Parish of Friern Barnet" in 1783. He was a distant relative of the Bacon who may or may not have written Shakespeare's plays. When he died in 1816, he held 651 acres of which 139 were in his own name together with other holdings in Finchley and East Barnet, and he owned Friary Park. 182 acres were held by his son John William who lived at Manor Farm (now the North Middlesex Golf Club), 138 were leased to John Gaywood and the rest were held by smaller tenants. On Bacon's death he left a financial tangle, because he had borrowed money to help pay the costs of the Enclosure provisions of January 1816, and after an action in the Court of Chancery the estate had to be sold at auction. Bacon's tomb is in St James's churchyard close to the entrance porch.

About 81 acres of the estate were bought by Thomas Bensley who planned to use them to build a lunatic asylum there, but he went bankrupt and the estate was further divided.

99. St John's Church in about 1900. Street lights and trams have not yet arrived.

FRIARY PARK

Friary Park may well be the site of the earliest settlement in Friern Barnet. The parish church of St James is first mentioned in 1198 and such houses as there were would have been clustered nearby. The old road once called Avern Street ran past the estate and the south facing land would have been attractive to early farmers. The Dean and Chapter of St Paul's Cathedral, who were lords of the manor in 1551, erected a manor house here which became Friary or Friern House. The main entrance in Friern Barnet Lane and the tree lined avenue leading to the parish church have survived in much altered form. It is thought that Sir Walter Raleigh once lived here, hence the naming of nearby Raleigh Drive. By the time of the 1665 Hearth Tax, its owner, Sir William Gomvill, was taxed for 17 hearths.

The estate was bought by E.W. Richardson who began development in 1871, but in 1909 much of the grounds were bought for use as a public park by Friern Barnet District Board with financial help from Sydney Simmons JP.

St John's School in Crescent Road is the second to bear that name. St John's infants' school was opened in Glenthorne Road in 1884 and St John's National School was added next door in 1890. In spite of having additional classrooms it was all out of date by the 1960s and the St John's Church of England School was opened in Crescent Road in 1969. Friern Barnet County School was opened on a 3½-acre site in Hemington Avenue in 1960/61. It was intended to replace the senior section of Holly Park School.

JOHN MILES

The Manor Farm of 29 acres was bought in 1851 by John Miles for £6,000. He substantially rebuilt the residence and renamed it Manor House, and eventually he owned all the land from Friern Barnet Lane as far as Oakleigh Road North. The original farm house is first mentioned in 1661, and was large enough in 1777 to allow for several rooms to be sub-let to the Rector.

Miles was a director of the New River Company which, in the seventeenth century, had brought fresh water from Hertfordshire to London. In 1851 he gave the money to build a new St James's school next to the almshouses in Friern Barnet Lane, which is still in use as a nursery school. He contributed to the restoration of St James's church, and he also put up the money to build an infant school on the corner of Sherwood Street. After his widow's death in 1902, 35 acres were sold to the National Land Corporation to build Myddelton Park (named after the founder of the New River), Loring and Pollard Roads.

100. *Friern House, also known as Friary Park.*

101. *Friern Manor Farm was bought by John Miles in 1851. It is now occupied by the North Middlesex Golf Club.*

102. John Miles rebuilt the Manor Farm house in 1861. Confusingly, he renamed it Friern Manor House.

103. John Miles.

104. The lodge to John Miles's Manor House, which still survives. It was lived in by one of his coachmen.

105. A bedroom at Miles's Manor House c.1885.

After the death of John Bacon (see above), his daughter Maria, wife of Sir William Johnston, inherited Friern Lodge and 234 acres. This was sold after her death in 1847. The largest part, Frenchman's Farm, was named after Pierre Baume who came to England *c.*1825 and bought the farm in 1852. He moved to the Isle of Man where he died in 1875, aged 78 and the farm buildings were then described as two dilapidated weatherboarded cottages and barns. At that time the farm was valued at £40,000, which he left to various children's charities in the Isle of Man.

Bethune Park was used by Friern Barnet District Council as a landfill refuse dump and in 1939 the brick building next to the running track was built as a mortuary and gas cleansing station.

ST JAMES'S CHURCH

The parish church of St James contains some Norman work. A vestry was added in 1807 and the tower was reduced in 1812. When the church was restored and enlarged in 1853 the architects were the Habershon brothers, who also designed St James's School. The octagonal parish room, a striking feature, dates from 1978.

The North Middlesex Golf Club was formed in 1907 as a limited company owning some 74 acres. This land was bought by the Council in 1928 and leased back to the club.

Blackett's Brook, first mentioned in 1513, rises on the golf course and runs through Friary Park where it enters a culvert which eventually comes out in Pymmes Brook. Ruffins Bridge across the brook was probably a wooden foot bridge named after a local land owner who also had Ruffins Mead. It was decayed by 1519 and may have been rebuilt, as another name to be found later is Stone Bridge.

ALMSHOUSES AND SCHOOLS

Friern Barnet almshouses were paid for by Lawrence Campe and opened in 1612 in a field called Thromers or Tromers, possibly a local landowner whose arms are incorporated in the centre of the building. A large upstairs room at the end was set aside for twice daily prayers, and underneath was a room for "the common use of the alms people to bake, brew, wash and do other necessary work".

106. *Old St James's church, c.1779.*

107. *New St James's church c.1905.*

108. The ladies of the North Middlesex Golf Club, in 1926.

The first school in the district for 12 boys aged 6 to 9 and 12 girls aged 6 to 12, opened in an upstairs room of the almshouses. They were to be taught to read the bible and the girls received instruction in "good, plain needlework", by Mrs Earp, widow of the parish clerk who was engaged to teach at £10 per annum. After a few months she was given permission to teach arithmetic as well and was paid an extra £2 per year for doing so.

St James's School was built in 1853 on glebe land immediately to the south of the almshouses with money provided by John Miles and Joseph Baxendale. The head teacher was dismissed for drunkenness in 1896, and his successor wrote of the boys throwing stones and firing cap guns in the classroom. After a couple of years, however, the Inspector described it as a "model village school". After 1951, when Queenswell school was opened, the old building was used as a nursery school.

Friern Barnet infant school was also paid for by John Miles and built at the corner of Sherwood Road in 1859. The first teacher was Miss Marion Head, aged 20, who had five years' experience as a pupil teacher and was assisted by her younger sister aged 13. Their combined salary was £30 per annum with the use of the house and coal provided – later they were provided with free gas.

Because the school is actually in the parish of St John's, it was closed in 1883 and the site is now a printing works.

LOCAL HISTORY

In 1999 the Friern Barnet and District Local History Society was formed and by May 2001, had a membership of about 70. Its founder was John Donovan, who had lived in the area for some thirty years and, alarmed by the changes occurring, felt that an attempt should be made to record its history. The Society aims to record the history of all local clubs and societies, famous residents, local architecture and make recordings of the reminiscences of elderly residents.

109. *The Lawrence Campe almshouses, c.1905.*

110. *St James's National School, built in 1853 to the south of the almshouses.*

Colney Hatch and New Southgate

An early name for part of this district was Sarners or Sarnes Barnet, though its exact location is a mystery. Because it consisted of dense woodland on heavy clay soil it was not attractive to early settlers and in Norman times the population would have been sparse.

Much of the area consisted of the manor of Halliwick, first mentioned about 1280. This extended along the south side of Friern Barnet Road from Finchley to Betstyle and in 1810 was said to cover about 350 acres. George Smith, who died in 1847, had bought 119 acres and these lands, which included the manor house, passed to his son Henry Smith, who died in 1868.

Halliwick manor house and its grounds, built about 1602, stood south of the junction of Colney Hatch Lane and Woodhouse Road covering what is now Lyndhurst, Ferncroft, Hollickwood and Thurlestone Avenues. The estate ran as far as Muswell Hill. The house was described as an L-shaped building with one wing of two storeys

and the other of three. By 1897 it had 46 rooms in addition to outbuildings which included a gymnasium. The grounds of 22 acres included a lake and a garden famous for its vines. The house passed to the Hill family and Constance Hill ran a girls' school there in 1900, but Jelks bought it to use as a furniture store in 1918 and it gradually became more and more dilapidated until it was sold in 1932 to Oldham Estates. This land is now St Johns, Hollyfield and Hillside Avenues.

There were two early routes in the district. The main road to the North running along Colney Hatch and Friern Barnet Lanes formed the western boundary. Betstyle, which forms the eastern boundary, is mentioned in 1005 as Bettas Stygle. The second road ran east-west from Betstyle to Finchley. There is little settlement on either road shown on Roque's map surveyed about 1750.

COLNEY HATCH ASYLUM

The Great Northern Railway from King's Cross to the North was opened in 1850 with a station built specially to serve the Middlesex County Pauper Lunatic Asylum at Colney Hatch, which was opened a year later – there was a siding connecting with a light railway running up a ramp into the grounds of the asylum.

The foundation stone for what was usually

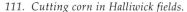

111. Cutting corn in Halliwick fields.

112. *Colney Hatch Lane in 1905. The cottages were accidentally burned down in 1909 by Robert Paul during the making of an adventure film.*

113. *The Middlesex Pauper Lunatic Asylum, also called Colney Hatch Asylum, as depicted in the Illustrated London News 12 May 1849.*

114. The laundry room at the Asylum.

called the Colney Hatch Asylum was laid by the Prince Consort in 1849 and the first patients were admitted on 17 July 1851. The opening of this institution was a historic step forward in the treatment of mental illnesses. In Hogarth's time a popular Sunday afternoon entertainment was to go to the Bethlem (or Bedlam) Hospital to laugh at the lunatics, whose treatment included being chained up, flogged and doused in cold water. From the inception at Colney Hatch it was the intention to treat patients with kindness and dignity. Previously mentally ill patients had been lumped together with other paupers in the local workhouse.

The site of 140 acres was chosen partly because it was airy and well drained but also because it was to be next to the new railway. Of this site, Mary Anne Curtis and her son Sir William Curtis had sold 119 acres to Middlesex in 1846.

The architect was S.W. Daukes (1811-1880). His training was with the York firm of Watson & Pritchett whose work had included West Riding County Lunatic Asylum in 1848. He practised mainly in Gloucester and Cheltenham specializing in railway stations and churches, including St Andrew's in Wells Street, in central London,

which was pulled down and reassembled at Kingsbury in 1933. It may be that his connections with the railways helped him to get the contract for Colney Hatch.

The brief was to design a hospital for 2,000 patients and 1,000 staff. The frontage of the building was 1,888 feet long. Some ten million bricks were dug and fired locally. There had been a previous tradition in the design of workhouses which dictated that wards and workshops should run at right angles to a main corridor, and as it was decided to build no higher than two storeys most wards and workshops on the ground floor opened off the longest corridor in Europe. In all, there were some six miles of wards and corridors and there was also a long service tunnel directly beneath the main corridor. The frontage, a gem of Victorian architecture, was about 1884 feet long.

The total cost was about £3,000,000 or £233 per patient.

Of the first patients some were just infirm physically or mentally handicapped, or just senile and no longer able to look after themselves. There were some blind patients and there were others with melancholia (now called depression).

The most common cause of melancholia in the 1850s amongst women was breakdown of marriage or death of a close relation, and in men the causes were fear of unemployment. Some 40-60% of this category of patients were discharged within six months.

Some 19% of all patients died there each year. There was a private burial ground on the site just to the right of the main entrance. In all 2,696 patients were buried there between 1851 and 1873. The stone recording this fact was removed after 1959 in order to modernize the image of the place. After 1873 patients were buried in the Great Northern Cemetery. Post mortems were carried out on some patients in order to understand mental and brain conditions more fully.

The story of one patient is told in *Psychiatry for the Poor* by Richard Hunter and Ida MacAlpine. Mary Beard was number 876 in the female case books. She was admitted in 1852 at the age of 10 and died in 1877 aged 25. She had had fits from the age of 12 months and suffered from the resultant behaviour disorders. She supported her mother and three sisters by entertaining in pubs, presumably because she was the eldest. Of "weak intellect but clever with numbers", she was prone to mood swings and periods of "religiosity". Her autopsy report reported:

> Died... from Exhaustion from Pulmonary Consumption with Diarrhoea which came on rather rapidly during the past six months. She had occasional attacks of Diarrhoea with much pain which yielded to treatment. The lungs became severely affected with rapid emaciation. She had not had attacks of epilepsy so severe during the late years. She was educated in the asylum and became much attached to the place ... and afforded much assistance to the Assistant Matrons in making out papers and calling over the numbers for the articles required in the ward in the store rooms. She was also very orderly and regular except during her epileptic fits in taking up the letter bag and giving messages in the different parts of the asylum.

The asylum produced 100,000 gallons of sewage daily which went at first direct into Strawberry Brook, then to Pymmes Brook and thence down to Edmonton where the inhabitants were not amused, and to alleviate this a large sewage farm was built which discharged clean water.

An agricultural farm, run largely by the inmates, was opened in 1858 so that the asylum could produce enough food to be self-supporting. In 1909 there were 8 horses, 65 cows, 2 bulls, 10 heifers, 10 calves, 397 pigs, 60 sheep, 350 fowls and 4 ferrets. Vegetables were grown and by 1900 there was a profit of £300 on farm produce.

In 1853 it was reported that 75 men were employed on the farm and 144 in the workshops, 62 women worked in the laundry, 56 in the kitchen, 96 helped with cleaning, 151 did needlework and 11 fancy work. The whole of the baking and brewing was done by the patients with the assistance of only two paid staff. Cooking by gas instead of coal was introduced in 1860 when the nearby gas works came into full production. In 1871 the Rev Henry Hawkins, chaplain to the Asylum, began to campaign for the "Aftercare of Poor and Friendless Convalescents on leaving the Asylums for the Insane". In 1888, when there were five doctors for 2,500 patients, groups of up to 200 men were taken for country walks and some 50 women were also taken out.

In 1896 a temporary building of wood and iron for 320 women was made in order to reduce overcrowding. The Commissioners for Lunacy expressed concern over a possible fire risk and this was borne out in 1903 when 51 patients were killed in the worst fire in the history of English hospitals.

A number of troops used the hospital to recover from wounds in the First World War. In the Second World War one female villa was destroyed by bombs on 26 October 1940, with the loss of four lives. On 16 November a land mine destroyed numbers 4, 5 and 6 female villas with four deaths. 624 beds there were reserved for the emergency services under the medical direction of St Bartholomew's Hospital and the Home Guard had a rifle range in the grounds. On 22 Jan 1945 a long-range rocket landed in the grounds 300 yards from Colney Hatch Lane and 20 yards from the North Circular Road. There was superficial damage to the hospital and nearby houses.

The term 'Asylum' had been dropped in 1930, and in 1959 when the Mental Health Act came into operation the building was renamed Friern Hospital. In 1967 the weekly cost of each patient was £13 9s 4d.

As a result of the 1983 Mental Health Act a ten-year closure programme was begun and the hospital closed on 31 March 1993. Since then the main building has been converted into apartments and the remaining land sold to build a shopping park.

THE HOLLY PARK ESTATE

The asylum created about a thousand jobs and this, coupled with the proximity of a railway station, was a stimulus to local house building. George Knights Smith (died 1886) another member of a confusing family, began laying out the Holly Park estate of 33 acres in 1879, north of Friern Barnet Road, west of the railway and near to New Southgate station. The houses were described as 'smart villas' often semi-detached or in rows of terraced three-storey houses, frequently with attractive names like Edith, Thorne or Glen Villas or Clydesdale Terrace. There was an attempt to brighten up the appearance by adding mouldings which have since often been picked out in colours. The estate was laid out in 424 plots forming, amongst others, Beaconsfield and Glenthorne Roads. Sewers were dug in 1879 but by that time only 47 houses had been built. The roads were fully built up by about 1897 though the road surfaces were not made up until 1910.

The Holly Park estate was formerly farm land which, until the Reformation, was owned by the Cistercian order of monks. The main crop was grass to feed London's thousands of horses, but there were a few cows, pigs and especially sheep for local use. The local vegetation can be deduced from field names like Long Meadow, Burnt Tree Field, Dung Field, Thistly Field, Rye Grass Field and Ruffins Meadow.

The Incognito Theatre was built out of a disused soda syphon factory in Holly Park Road largely as a result of the enthusiasm of Douglas Weatherhead, its sometime leading actor or director. It was there that David Jason (born David White in Finchley in 1940), who had attended Northside School, made his stage debut. He was praised by Bill Gelder, doyen of local critics for the energy and ability of his performance in *Journey's End* by R.C. Sherriff in December 1957. Jason went on to star in numerous television classics, particularly *Only Fools and Horses*. He is now patron of the Incognitos.

Holly Park School was the first council school in the district and built in spite of opposition from the churches who wanted to keep control of education. It was opened in 1908 for 300 juniors and extended in 1915 to include infants. The first head teacher, W.G. Collier, unusually for the time, believed that if children understood what they were doing they would be more likely to remember. He urged co-operation rather than fear as a way of keeping discipline. By 1945 it had

115. *The scholarship boys of Holly Park school in 1915.*

become a mixed senior school teaching pupils up to the age of 14 and by 2001 there were about 400 pupils organised into 12 classes.

At the corner of Friern Barnet Road and Oakleigh Road South cottages were being let for rent in 1854 in Carlisle Place. The Avenue was laid out about 1890 by the United Estates and Investment Company, as were St Paul's, Holmesdale and Stanhope Roads. This was considered to be one of the roughest parts of the district– in 1883 there were 925 inhabitants living in only 185 houses. These roads disappeared when the district was rebuilt after 1969 when Link Road was made up and Coppies Grove and blocks of modern flats were built.

Christ Church URC was founded in a lecture hall on the corner of Bellevue and Friern Barnet Roads about 1884. A church designed by George Baines & Co. was added in 1910. Like the hall, it is of red brick with stone dressings.

The first minister was Benjamin Waugh (1839 to 1908). He was born at Settle in Yorkshire and educated for the Congregational Ministry. He was minister in Newbury and Greenwich before moving to Friern Barnet in 1885 to 1887. In partnership with John 'Rob Roy' McGregor, he founded a day Institute for Wastepaper and Blacking Boys where they were educated. He formed a connection with two deep sea fishing boat owners who offered employment to the lads. In 1884 he formed the London Society for the Prevention of Cruelty to Children in 1889. His attempts to improve the lot of neglected children were aided by the Chief Rabbi of the day and the Catholic Cardinal Manning.

He was an adviser to Parliament for the 1889 Act concerned Cruelty to Children, which established the legal right for children to be fed, clothed

116. The former Freehold Social Institute, which held regular coffee evenings before the First World War. It is now used for light industry.

and properly treated, and made provision for children to be taken away from neglectful parents. He was an admirable public speaker, equally effective in committee. He retired to Westcliffe on Sea through ill health in 1905 and is buried in Southend.

THE FREEHOLD ESTATE

The Freehold estate was centred on Sydney Road and covered much of what is now Cromwell and Hampden Roads. It was laid out about 1863 by the Westminster Freehold Land Society on low, badly-drained land close to Strawberry Brook. But it was built with very limited public services such as sewage disposal and road upkeep. By 1867 overcrowding was such that there were about a thousand people living in 130 houses, many of them labourers attracted by employment at Alexandra Palace. Seven inhabitants per house was about the average in that year.

Sydney Road has a mixture of Victorian terraced houses and semis built in the 1930s – no. 33 is the most unusual bungalow on the estate. A bus garage, opened in 1931 at 165 Sydney Road, next to the school, has been succeeded by a block of flats. A second bus depot was opened at much the same time in Hampden Road between nos. 52 and 58. Haldane Close in Cromwell Road was built in the early 1970s.

Slum clearance in the area was proposed as long ago as 1933, but new flats were not built in Hampden Road until 1975 and Pert Close, a large estate of 3-storey flats, was erected *c.*1970. The name of the nearby Freehold Community Centre

is the only link with the early days of the development. Hollickwood Park is built on the former council refuse tip.

Sydney Road school was built in 1906 to take infants from the nearby St Peter's school and by 1914 had accommodation for 299 pupils. By 1936 there were 524 places in a junior mixed and infant school. Renamed Hollickwood in 1938, it was demolished in 1974.

Robert Paul bought land in Sydney Road in 1897 to build a film studio. He transferred his instrument workshop from Hatton Garden to Sydney Road in 1903 where he specialised in the manufacture of measuring instruments such as thermometers. By then much extended, the factory closed in 1975. In 1920 the firm had become the Cambridge Instrument Company which, in 1974, was taken over by Brown Boveri, a Swiss firm. At its peak they employed about 750 people. Cambridge Close is built on the site and Robert Paul's house at no. 49 now has a blue plaque.

In *c.*1894 Paul and his partner, Birt Acres, discovered that Edison had neglected to patent his kinetoscope in England and set about making a machine to show 40-second films. Their first effort looked rather like the peep-show machines familiar on seaside piers. Together they made a motion picture camera which they used to record the Boat Race and the Derby – the 1895 race was shown at the Alhambra Music Hall within 24 hours of the event, when the audience cheered and the orchestra played 'God Bless the Prince of Wales'. Paul next turned his attention to trick photography. The film *A runaway motor car through Piccadilly Circus* used the technique of turning the crank slowly and playing back at normal speed.

St Peter's church began life in a hut and then in a corrugated-iron building. Work on a more permanent church was financed by the sale of St Peter-le-Poer in the City in 1909, when many items such as silver-gilt chalices, patens, flagons and alms dishes, the pulpit, bells, organ, font etc, were transferred to the new building. The architect was W.D. Caröe (1857-1938), who also built the Working Men's College in Camden Town and St Luke's church in Finchley.

The land to the west of Friern Barnet Lane formed the southernmost part of the Halliwick estate and was used by Muswell Hill Farm and Coppetts Farm in 1894. Development of this began in 1969.

The Albion Estates Company developed Albion Road, George Crescent and Halliwick Road around 1899.

West Finchley and Woodside Park

Nether Street ran on the nether or far side of the Finchley Common. Probably medieval in origin, it is first mentioned in 1365.

Elm Grange and Elm Villa, two houses which existed here by 1720, were pulled down in 1824 and replaced by Brent Lodge, the home of Francis Hamilton, whose family name is remembered in nearby Hamilton Way. In turn Brent Lodge was demolished in 1905 and replaced by Cedar Court by 1935. However, its two entrance lodges remain, one in Finchley Way and the other in Pentstemon Close. The Hamilton family also owned Falkland House in Ballards Lane.

F.A. Hamilton was born in 1814 in Staffordshire. He entered the banking world in 1832, rose rapidly, went to America to study their methods and returned to England in 1845 to become a partner in Brown, Shipley & Co. At the 1881 census he and his wife had a butler, two footmen, a groom, a coachman, a cook, a lady's maid, a parlour maid, a housemaid an under housemaid, a kitchen maid and a scullery maid.

The Hamiltons gave a thousand pounds, more than half the purchase price, to buy the Queen Victoria Diamond Jubilee Park off Ballards Lane in 1897, and they also gave money towards the Wesleyan church in Ballards Lane, St Paul's church in Long Lane, Christ Church on Finchley Common, the Wright-Kingsford Home, the Finchley Cottage Hospital and many other charities.

Confusingly, another Elm Grange was built on the east side of Nether Street. In 1894 this was sold by Edward Tewart to James Williamson, a developer, of Grove Villas, Finchley and its site is now covered by Sellars Hall flats. Elm Park Road, Eversleigh Road, Grosvenor Road and Lansdown Road had all been laid out by 1896 and built up in ten years.

Much of this area, to the west of the High Barnet branch of the Northern line, was taken up by Fursby House and a farm of about 40 acres running down to the Dollis Brook. It was used as a nursery by William Batho who went bankrupt in 1902. The house stood almost exactly where Fursby Avenue is now. The whole estate was developed for housing about 1933.

117. *A house in Nether Street, depicted in* The Builder *in February 1883. It was built for a Miss T. Boulton, and the architect was Thomas Newell.*

". . . the House is a sound financial proposition . . . . . . it will improve in value—" *this is what a leading architect says about* **WOODSIDE PARK —.**

All the houses on the Estate are built to the same standard of quality with large rooms and extensive gardens. Every house embodies the requirements of modern living and is equipped for minimum labour and maximum comfort —— and is definitely inexpensive to run.

See our new **"ESTATE PICTORIAL"**

ARCHITECTURAL SERVICE

Our architectural office is always ready to give advice on matters of construction and design, and will be only too glad to design a house embodying your own ideas. A Home built to your own design can be purchased on exactly the same terms as other houses at Woodside Park.

NO Road, Legal or Survey Charges

HOUSES FROM £950 to £1,800

WOODSIDE PARK

GARDEN SUBURB ALEXANDRA GROVE, FINCHLEY, N.12

★ **Send this Coupon to-day** *for* or Phone Finchley 4182 **NEW ESTATE PICTORIAL**

WOODSIDE PARK GARDEN SUBURB
Woodside Park Station nearby.
Buses 2, 26, 84 and trams from Paddington, Cricklewood and Golders Green stop close by.

Name..

Address..

.... F.P.

1936

118. A 1936 advertisement for new houses in Woodside Park.

119. *Cedar Court in Nether Street, was built in the 1930s on the site of Frederick Hamilton's Brent Lodge.*

Jersey Farm was to the north, between Nether Street and the Brook by 1887. With 100 cows, it was one of the largest dairy farms in the district. Gone by 1920, it is now covered by Westbury Road, Spring Close and surrounding roads.

Court House, at the northern end of Nether Street, owned by the Peacock family about 1664, was probably the court house of Frith Manor. When William Leader died in 1829 the lands and house went to his son John who in turn sold them to a Mrs Burridge who sold them for building in 1936. The farm house was a red brick building extended in 1863 by Samuel Wimbush, the then tenant. It was partly demolished in 1927 and completely in 1936. For many years some of the buildings were used by Sandwell Ladies' College. Gainsborough Court and 200 acres were leased to Jersey Farm. Courthouse Farm Dairy had a shop in Prince's Parade, Church End in 1906.

To the west of the Brook, the Southover and Northiam estates were laid out on part of Laurel Farm from 1935 onwards and Tillingham Way was developed by 1938. This district was Longcroft or Longland in 1640. Longland Drive, Hill Crescent, Laurel Drive and Green Way were partly complete by 1936; in 1935 Ventnor Drive had houses at both ends with a field in the middle. Woodridge School was planned in 1938 but was delayed by the war and changes in development plans. It was finally opened in 1967.

120. *Argyle Road in 1900.*

North Finchley

Between the High Road and the south side of Woodhouse Road was the Churchfield estate which had only one house on it in 1895 before it was laid out for housing in 1900. Christ Church, on the east side of the High Road was built in 1864 when the London Diocesan Mission arranged for the Revd Henry Stephens to work among the navvies who were constructing the railways in the locality. Their temporary iron building was replaced by the present stone church in 1869. Designed by J. Norton, it was extended in 1874 and 1880 when south and north aisles were added. The elaborate vicarage was pulled down in the 1990s and replaced by Hamilton Court, a block of privately owned flats, named after one of the church's benefactors.

Stephens, who died in 1898, was very active in his parish and arranged for missions to open in Percy Road (1899), Holden Road (1885-1909) and Summers Lane (1906-1960). To mark his work, the Stephens Memorial Hall, which included a library, was built on the corner of Stanhope Road and High Road, north of Tally Ho Corner. It later became a cinema called the Stanhope. The *Finchley*

122. *Christ Church.*

Press in 1910 reported "For up-to-dateness the new picture hall in North Finchley would be hard to beat. Last night within a few hours of the event, pictures of the funerals of the policemen who lost their lives in the East End last week were being shown in this hall. The Stanhope Hall has been entirely redecorated. It is lit by electricity,

121. *The Stephens Memorial Hall at the junction of High Road and Castle Road.*

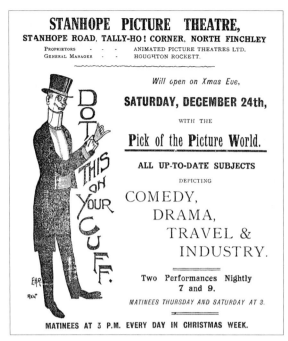

123. *Christmas Eve entertainment at the Stanhope in 1910.*

draughts are impossible while fine leather tip up seats have been provided.

Refreshments are provided on a liberal scale, while vocal selections were provided by 'Little Thomas' late of Mowhawk's Minstrels.''

On the western side of Ballards Lane, the Moss Hall estate was developed from 1867. Moss Hall itself (demolished 1927) was a large house standing back from Nether Street. The name probably comes from John Mosse, who was a tenant of the Bishop of London in 1484. By the next year his name had become Mos in available records and by 1609 it was Mowse. The site was bought by the Goodyear family in 1824, but they had to go to Chancery to obtain possession. It is not known when the old house was actually demolished. Moss Hall Grove and Moss Hall Terrace were built by 1880.

Finchley Education Committee began planning a new school at Moss Hall in December 1946, though it was not opened until 1952. The former Moss Hall site was cleared and separate two-form entry infants and junior schools were built, together with a 60-place nursery.

Alexandra Grove was named after the Queen. Mrs Marshman ran a ladies' college in Alexandra

House in 1881, later taken over by Miss Rhoda Gynne. The college was typical of many establishments of the period. In 1881 Mrs Marshman, a widow of 57, was assisted by a German governess aged 30, and French, English and Music governesses each aged 20. The pupils were all boarders and included 9 wards of court (orphans?) and seventeen other pupils aged from 10 to 19, eight of whom were daughters of officers serving abroad.

The college has since been demolished and is now Phillipson House.

Leases for building in nearby Hutton Grove and Dale Grove were granted from 1873. A day and Sunday school were built in Dale Grove in 1864 with money donated by J.H. Puget. The day school was planned for 40 infants and 40 older children, but by 1870 the average attendance was 64 infants and 93 older children. The building was sold to the Baptists in 1893.

An earlier church called the Cottager's Chapel had been built by T.C. Newman in the grounds of his house Orchard Lodge, which stood on a site later to became the Gaumont Cinema between Ballards Lane and Great North Road. He was pastor from 1837 until 1866. His chapel accommodated about eighty.

Finchley Common Congregational Church was built in Nether Street in 1864 on land again given by J.H. Puget. Designed by Messrs Searle, it was opened in 1865.

Two large Victorian houses, Inglenook and The Grange in Nether Street were bought for the Sisters of the Poor Child Jesus at St Michael's Convent and Schools in 1908. Most of the site is now used by St Michael's Catholic Grammar School.

TRAMS

The coming of electric trams in 1905 revolutionised the district by providing cheap and quick travel to London. A tram depot was opened at the junction of Christchurch Avenue and Woodberry Grove in 1905/6. Route 19 ran from Barnet to Highgate along the Great North Road; no. 21 went from Finchley along Woodhouse Road to Bounds Green and Finsbury Park and eventually to Holborn, while routes 45 and 60 ran along Ballards Lane and past Golders Green.

In order to reach the depot, trams from London had to run past the junction with Ballards Lane and then cross the on coming traffic and then along Ballards Lane.

TALLY HO CORNER

There were three Tally Ho coaches which ran from London to Birmingham. They were the Patent Tally Ho which was horsed by P. Nelson as far as South Mimms, the Independent Tally Ho run by Horne, and the Eclipse Tally Ho, owned in 1823 by a Mrs Mountain. The Eclipse was described (perhaps by a jealous rival) as a "a tawdry thing all flaunting with green and gold compared with a royal simplicity of form and colour". The three coaches were said to be the fastest in England. They were timed at 10 mph and covered the 119 miles to Birmingham in 11 hours and 56 minutes.

The triangular site formed by the junction of Ballards Lane and High Road has undergone many changes over the years. By the end of the nineteenth century the apex at the north was occupied by the Park Road Hotel, renamed later the Tally Ho (which was rebuilt in 1927). South of that were stables and a smithy. The southern end of the site was formed by an extension of Nether Street, which today is taken by the bus stand. To improve access to the tram depot, Woodhouse Road was extended to form the Kingsway in 1934, thereby pushing the whole road system further south. A row of shops with accommodation above, called Market Parade was built in the High Road north of the junction with Woodhouse Road about 1905. The National Provincial Bank had the place of honour in the centre. The land had been owned by the Ball family which sold it in 1892 to the Revd E. Castle.

MORE CINEMAS

The Grand Hall Cinema was built by Ashby's New Halls Ltd and opened in Market Parade in 1911. The cinema, enlarged in 1918, was bought in 1922 by the National Electric Theatre Company which had links with Gaumont British. The Grand Hall closed in 1937.

Miss Fanny Kitson had been in service with the Ball family who lived in Boreham Wood. She was helped by her employers to buy a shop at 14 Market Parade next to the Grand Hall for use as a café. It proved to be very profitable so much so that, having married Mr E. Hudgell, projectionist at the Grand, she was able to buy the site of the cinema.

During the last war the cinema was used as a furniture store, but it was demolished in 1957 and its site is now used by Radio Rentals.

The Gaumont Cinema opened opposite the Grand Hall in 1937 on a site created by the construction of Kingsway. It had a spacious foyer so that patrons could queue under cover and a large restaurant on the first floor. The organ was salvaged when the cinema was demol-

124. The High Road looking south towards Tally Ho Corner c.1905. At that time the site of the today's Tally Ho was occupied by the Park Road Hotel.

125. *A tram at Kingsway shortly after the road was built in 1934. The site of Orchard Lodge, later to be the Gaumont cinema, is being cleared on the left.*

126. *The Grand Hall cinema in the High Road. The cinema was superseded by the new Gaumont cinema, which was built opposite.*

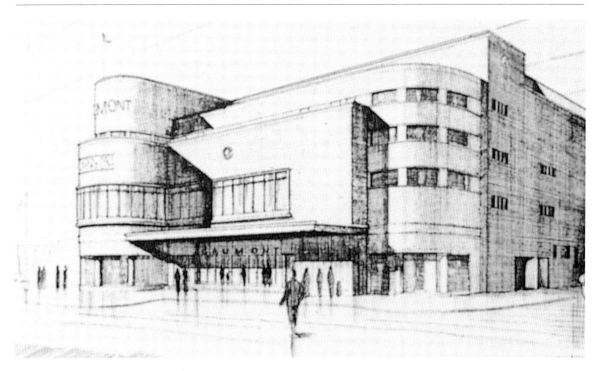

127. *The Gaumont Cinema, opened in 1937.*

128. *Auditorium of the Gaumont.*

129. Opening night at the Gaumont in 1937.

ished and is now an attraction in a pub at Great Munden in Hertfordshire.

The site has been earmarked as a possible borough arts centre. Until that happens it is empty and is used as a street market.

WARTIME FRICTION

War against Germany was declared on 12 August 1914. In the anti-German campaign whipped up by some of the press, traders with Germanic names, whether they were German or not, were at risk from attacks from local population. One such was Harry Flach, a tobacconist and newsagent in Park Parade, North Finchley. The mob, as the *Finchley Press* reported, practically demolished his premises.

Stones and bricks were hurled and the glass front disappeared. There was plenty of ammunition at hand as Messrs Jelks were having a new warehouse erected nearby.

> Owing to a timely warning, Inspector Wallis and a number of constables from Church End soon appeared on the scene. They commandeered a tram and ordered the driver not to stop until he got to North Finchley. The occupiers of the flats above, good honest English folk, displayed a Union Jack and were left

unmolested. It is said that the cause of the whole business were the pro-German sentiments expressed by the man Flach. He denied this however saying that he was in fact a Russian Jew and a naturalised English subject.

After leaving Mr Flach's premises, the mob made a sudden dive for Mr Rissert's hairdresser's shop. Apparently they were under the misapprehension that Mr Rissert is a foreigner.

The following night (Saturday) was one of great excitement. From early on a large crowd gathered at North Finchley in the expectation of seeing more shops wrecked. Quite 200 police were on the scene and kept the spectators on the move, though people were crowded together as thickly as on Carnival Day. During the evening there were half a dozen arrests. There is no doubt that the presence of so many police officers prevented serious damage to shops.

At Highgate Court, Charles Cooper and James Butcher of Friern Park, North Finchley were charged with committing damage to windows. Frederick Cox and Thurza Cox, his wife, of Percy Road were charged with disorderly conduct. Sgt Floyd said that he asked the accused to move on. The woman refused and struck him on the head with both hands knocking his helmet off. John Cox of Grove Road was then charged with attempting to rescue Mrs Cox. Ernest Waghorn and Sidney Kirby, both of Swan Lane, were charged with drunkenness, disorderly conduct and using obscene language. All the above were fined 2s 6d and bound over to keep the peace.

A NEW SCHOOL

Christ Church National School opened in Stanhope Road in 1875, intended for 225 children. It had previously been a small infants' school in Lodge Lane. Much of the finance came from the vicar, the Revd Henry Stephens. The school was enlarged in 1904 and again in 1933 when it became a senior school and in 1944 became a secondary modern. It moved to a new building in Hilton Avenue in 1968 when there were about 450 pupils on the roll. The old buildings are used now as an Adult Education Institute.

The school log books illustrate very clearly the poor state of the early schools. In the infant classroom there were only three benches, very old and unsteady, intended to seat 18 children, one small cupboard for books and one rough dilapidated box for needlework. A third classroom measuring 12 feet by 10 feet contained 22 children standing round the wall at a scripture lesson. In that room there was no furniture at all except a blackboard without an easel and a paraffin stove which was not lighted and was said not to work anyway. "A horrible stench met me here in the open air some yards from the boy's urinal, arising I concluded from the latter not being washed down and the drain to it probably not acting. The smell was so bad that I was unable to examine it quite thoroughly."

The above is no particular criticism of Christ Church school – it is included as an example of the conditions under which many children of the period were educated.

William Jelks had opened a house furnishing store in the High Road by 1890. At that time he lived above the shop. By 1935 he had enlarged his business and opened a large storage warehouse (1914) behind the Tally Ho pub. He himself had moved to live more comfortably at The Grange in Whetstone.

A little farther north Robert Prior opened a drapery store (*see ill. 133*). After the demolition of the Stephens Memorial Hall (*see p91*) he had a new store built on the corner of Castle Road. Though much altered today, it retains some of the 1938 art deco style windows hidden behind modern display stands. Coathouse Farm stood just west of the junction of Nether Street and Gainsborough Road – Avondale Avenue now occupies its site.

Finchley Lodge stood at the end of Lodge Lane which was originally its driveway. The house probably dated back to 1610 when Henry Gerrard was fined for encroaching on the common with "rayles before his house". In 1621 he was permitted to "demise a messuage or tenement, a garden and an orchard".

The building was demolished about 1934 when massive Tudor timbers were uncovered and burned on site. The usual range of cellars gave rise to the usual range of rumours about secret passages.

130. Woodhouse Road c.1900 (see p.98).

WOODHOUSE ROAD

Ownership of property in the area known as the Woodhouses is mentioned in the will of Allan Brent in 1655. On 25 January 1762, Lawrence Cottam became the owner of the Woodhouse estate which he left in his will of 19 May 1775 to his nephew George. By 19 May 1784 the estate had passed to Thomas Collins (through his wife) and is described as "land near the Woodhouse field heretofore waste, and also one of the Woodhouses on the way leading from the Great North Road to Colney Hatch". The same document refers to "the mansion", now known as Woodhouse, whose rateable value increased from £26 in 1784 to £50 in 1798. Collins was "an Artist, craftsman and ornamental plasterer". Some of his work has survived in the present building, now the Woodhouse College, at the bend of Woodhouse Road just before Hilton Avenue. Later owners included Margaret Collins who, in August 1830, leased for one year "all that freehold messuage known as Woodhouse with outbuildings and appurtenances". The occupants in 1830 are shown as J. Collins, J. Barclay and O. Delano, all tenants. The 1841 census has William Lambert, of independent means, there with his wife

Margaret and five servants. Lambert Road is named after this family.

A map of 1880 shows the road curving around the building and its front yard, with a pond on the other side named Hogman's Hern. According to Reaney's *Origin of English Place Names*, 'Hern' is a corruption of heron and often refers to a fish pond visited by herons. However another dictionary of place names says 'hern' means corner. A large house like Woodhouse would have had a fish pond.

Some time around 1880, there was a short-lived school in the building. It was a 'crammer' specialising in the preparation of boys for entrance exams for the professions and the services. It had a staff of two, Mr Laughton, the Head, and a maths tutor. The 1881 census records that two families of gypsies lived in the grounds. They were classified as 'sleepies' and were born in Hampshire. John Skelton, a coachman lived in the house later occupied by generations of school caretakers.

George Wright inherited the property on 29 April 1881 on condition that he changed his name to Wright-Ingle. By 1888 the house had been remodelled internally and took the form which

131. The drawing room of Woodhouse c.1914.

was later to become the core of Woodhouse School. In 1911, Thomas Needham was living at Woodhouse and the last private occupiers were the Busvine family.

WOODHOUSE SCHOOL
Classes from North Road Central School moved from the North Road site in East Finchley to Woodhouse Road on 1 December 1922. The school was renamed Woodhouse School on 1 September 1924. School fees were to be three guineas per term with 25% of the places being free. The first head teacher was E. Barlow Butlin whose salary in 1925 was £600 per year. In 1939 part of the basement was requisitioned as an emergency control centre and for a Bomb Disposal Unit which"trundled their awe inspiring trophies in and out of Room 1". As with most other schools, air raid shelters were dug in the field.

With the introduction of comprehensive schools in the 1970s the buildings became a sixth form college at which time there was an enormous expansion in facilities.

Ian Bedford is the school's most distinguished sportsman. He played cricket for Finchley and Middlesex. His Middlesex record was – batting 64 innings with an average of 15 and bowling 103 wickets at 32 runs a piece. He was a subtle leg spin bowler who did not quite achieve his promise, though he did play against the Australians and did captain Middlesex in 1961-2. He died at a tragically early age.

NORTH OF THE TALLY HO
North of Tally Ho Corner the opening of the railway station in 1872 (originally called Torrington Park and renamed Woodside Park in 1882), was the stimulus for house building. To the west of the railway line is Holden Road, in which stands St Barnabas, rebuilt in 1912 by J.S. Alder. It has splendid acoustics, being used by Finchley Choral Society and by major recording companies. This replaced a corrugated iron hut of 1885.

The nearby Albert Street School used a three decker building with the infants on the ground floor, the girls on the middle and the boys on the top floor. There was strong opposition from local churches to the opening of state schools and this was the first school built by the Finchley School Board. In September 1881 the staff and monthly salaries were:

132. Woodside Park station c.1905.

133. Prior's department store in North Finchley c.1936. This family-run business moved to the junction of the High Road and Castle Road shortly after this picture was taken. The second store was taken over by Owen Owen, but was closed in August 1993.

Mr Meggs, master £12.10.0d
Miss Boreham, infant mistress, £6.13.4d
Mr Gray, certificated teacher, £5.0.0d
Miss A. Stacey, pupil teacher (aged 18), £1.5.0d
Miss E. Ackhurst, pupil teacher, £1.0.0d
Miss E. Beak, pupil teacher, £1.0.0d
Miss M. Moore, pupil teacher (aged 15), 16s 8d
Mrs Potter, certificated teacher, £2.0.0d

Mr Meggs asked for an extra teacher as he and Mr Gray were teaching 160 boys between them.

The school was reorganised in 1923 into junior and senior departments with about a thousand children between them. The name was changed to Northside in 1932 and the senior department moved out in 1956 and eventually became part of Compton School in Summers Lane. By 2001 the Junior Mixed and Infants school had about 300 children on the roll including the Nursery.

134. The Torrington Arms c.1900.

A large detached house called 'Bianna' stood on the site of today's Sainsbury's in the High Road. In 1934 it was bought by George Sherwood and here he built premises for the Great Northern Motors which soon became the largest Austin garage in north London. Before Sainsbury's the Co-op had a store here. A stone denoting that it

is eight miles to London still remains outside.

The Torrington Arms was originally a coaching inn and horse bus stopping place and also a Post Office receiving office. It was rebuilt in 1900 and again in 1962, but the billiard saloon which once stood on its south side has now gone.

Just south of this Torrington Park was laid out by Henry Holden from 1872. Nos 32 and 34, with their coachhouse in between, are listed buildings as "an early nineteenth century pair", as are nos 36 and 38. Eric Morecambe lived in Torrington Park from 1956 until 1961. One of Britain's best loved comedians, his partnership with Ernie Wise was legendary and their Christmas television shows played to record audiences year after year.

North of Sainsbury's, in Ravensdale Avenue, the public library was opened by Finchley council in 1936.

Woodside Park Road leads directly to the station. Henry Holden, the estate developer, lived at Mosely Dene on the corner with Woodside Grange Road in a house that is now the International College. He named Holden Road after his family and built the Woodside Assembly Rooms opposite his house.

135. Eric Morecambe.

136. The public library in Ravensdale Avenue, opened in 1936.

137. No. 64 Friern Park, one of the roads probably developed by Henry Holden.

At the south corner of Frederick's Place, further north up the High Road, were Arlington Cottages, the nearest thing that early Finchley had to a police station.

Numbers 1 and 2 Frederick's Place are shown on the 1851 census as a Horse Patrol Station. Victoria Cottage, on the north side of the junction was occupied by John Smith, Superintendent, Bow Street Horse Patrol. He would have used his house as his office. Next door was Ralph Norman, police sergeant and next to him was John Summers, P C.

The duty roster dated 7 October 1836 for the patrol has survived:

Working from Finchley station.
P C 45   Joseph Higgs
P C 46   Robert Brofhaw
P C 47   Thomas North
P C 48   Samuel Collard
Working from Whetstone station
P C 49   John Smith
P C 50   William Davis

P C 45 worked or walked or rode Finchley New Road, a distance of 5° miles, Barnet Road to Grand Junction Gate two times and from the 4th milestone to the 5th milestone four times.

P C 46   Finchley New Road, Barnet Road, Grand Junction Gate a distance of 5° miles two times and from the 2nd to the 4th milestone four times.

P C 47 Barnet Road from the Wellington bar to Whetstone Gate, a distance of 4 miles twice and from the 6th to the 8th milestone four times.

P C 48 Barnet Road to the Wellington Bar at Barnet a distance of 5° miles two times and from the 9th to the 10th milestone four times.

P C 49 Barnet to Archway Highgate a distance of 6 mles two times and from the 8th to the 9th milestone four times

P C 50 Finchley New Road station to Grand Junction gate a distance of 6 miles and from the 3rd to the 4th milestone four times.

Part of the duties of each constable was to visit each pub on his beat four times a day.

When Arlington Cottages were demolished, an elaborately decorated police truncheon was discovered hidden up a chimney. Its present location is unknown.

Ebenezer Holman lived at Friern Watch opposite, a very large mansion standing well back from the east side of the High Road in substantial grounds. Interestingly, the Parliamentary constituency boundary shown on the 1894 map went straight through the middle of his house, and presumably he could vote differently if he were in his hallway or in his back sitting room. The same line also divided him between Finchley parish and Friern Barnet parish. He made his fortune as a boot manufacturer and left £324,000 on his death. He was a substantial local benefactor, giving the land for Finchley Cottage Hospital in 1908. His estate ran from what is now Ravensdale Avenue to Finchley Park where one of his entrance lodges still survives.

In the 1881 census he is shown with four daughters, who helped his wife run the house with the assistance of a butler, a cook, a housekeeper, five maids, a groom, a gardener and a lodge keeper. As an indication of how many people were moving into Finchley at this time, the census shows that although his family was born in Finchley, none of his ten servants was born anywhere near London. After his death his house was used by the All Saints Sisters as St Elizabeth's Home for Incurable Women. That in its turn has been demolished for housing developments.

Friern Watch is first recorded in 1580 when William Pert (died 13 Feb 1608) held the land on a 100-year lease from the Dean and Chapter of St Paul's Cathedral.

The Newcombe Estate Company began building houses in Friern Watch Avenue in 1914. In 1935 an Odeon Cinema was built in the High Road on part of the estate and history was made here in September 1937 when the first technicolour film in Finchley was shown. The site is now a Furniture Land shop.

Opposite Mayfield Avenue once stood a group of small houses called Waterloo Cottages. The *Finchley Press* in 1871 announced the death of one of their residents:

> Mr J Read, late of the 10th Royal Hussars of Waterloo Cottages, Whetstone died on 19 February 1871 aged 83. On one occasion at the Battle of Waterloo one of his whiskers was shot away by a ball which went on to kill his neighbour.

To the north was once a property called Finchley Park, also known as Goslings, held in 1486 by Thomas Sanny. The road called Finchley Park was begun in 1852. A roller skating rink opened in the High Road in 1910 opposite the site of the house. Although, or perhaps because, the rink had uniformed attendants and an orchestra, it was not a success and was soon closed and reopened as the Rink Cinema.

138. *Houses for sale in Mayfield Avenue in 1926.*

139. *The opening of the skating rink in North Finchley in 1910.*

140. The skating rink in the High Road.

The *Finchley Press* reported that "Pte Green of the Middlesex Regiment had both legs blown off in France on 13 November 1914; he had previously worked as an inside attendant and bill poster at the Rink Cinema."

The cinema was closed in 1923. Carrimore Six-Wheelers used the site as a lorry depot, which was in turn replaced by a police garage.

The Swan and Pyramids, on the west of the High Road, was before 1890 called the Swan with Two Necks. The latter name is a corruption and derived from the old custom of swan-upping which involved capturing the cygnets on the River Thames on the last Monday in July and cutting one nick in the bill if the bird belonged to the Company of Dyers, and two if it belonged to the Company of Vintners. Those swans belonging to the Crown were left unmarked.

Nearby were two ponds called Basings Ponds. Adam de Basing is shown owning land in Finchley in 1253. Possibly it was here that in 1615 Agnes Miller was punished. She had been prosecuted "for being a common scold and disturber of the neighbours and honest citizens of Finchley and Friern Barnet. It was ordered that the constables, headboroughs and other officers of Finchley and Friern Barnet to take the same Agnes to be duckt in some pond of water in or nere adioning to the said parishe in such sorte as common scolds are

wont to be".

The McCurd lorry factory was built on the corner of Woodside Grove and the High Road in 1915 making and repairing lorries for the war. Many of the 800 workers were women. It became a tradition that on Boxing Day there was a football match, men *vs* women, in which the men had to wear long, hobble skirts. The factory was taken over by De Dion, makers of back axles, and then by Burtonwood Engineering who were cylinder grinders. It was finally demolished in the 1950s.

Woodside Grange was a large house at the junction of Woodside Avenue and Woodside Lane owned by a Doctor Turle. Part of its site was taken by Finchley Catholic Grammar School in 1926. This became a direct grant independent school in 1939, a comprehensive in 1971 and is now Finchley Catholic High School, with some 650 students. An independent but linked preparatory school, St Albans's, was opened next door in 1945.

The east side of the site is occupied by the North London Hospice.

Terrace House is a fine Georgian property in Woodside Lane. The 1841 census has Edward Smith a Dissenting Minister living there. It was used by Simon Esting as a boarding school in 1841 and by 1871 it was sublet into three prop-

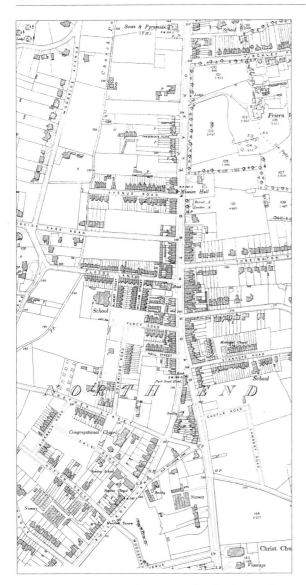

141. North Finchley in the 1890s with what is now the Tally Ho junction towards the bottom of the map.

142. The Swan and Pyramids in the High Road c.1900.

erties occupied by staff from Baxdendale's horse farm. By 1881 the quality of the house had been recognised. It was renovated and by 1892 was used by George Mainland, a solicitor.

A nice example of the rural nature of the district is this extract from the records of a local school in 1881:

> There was a stag hunt close to the school today. The stag, just before the afternoon school began, ran down Britannia Road. Shortly afterwards the men and dogs came along the High Road. This caused much excitement among the children. Seven came in too late to be marked present and four more played truant.

143. The High Road, Whetstone, about 1870.

Whetstone

THE EARLY VILLAGE

The place name Whetstone simply means West Town. Early forms include 'le Weston' (1398), 'Wheston' (1417) and 'Whetstonestret' (1439). The earliest settlement was near the church of St James in Friern Barnet Lane, but when the route across Finchley Common was changed after the Bishop of London opened a road across his land from Highgate, the village gradually moved north-west.

According to an indenture of 30 April 1650 Richard Uxber paid £337 4s 10d for

> ...all that Manor of Whetstone, also Friern Barnet with the right members and appurtenances, also all the quit rents of all the copyholders and customary tenants of the Manor, and all that Court Leet and View of Frank Pledge together with the perquisites and fees, late of the Dean and Chapter of St Paul's, and the Capital messuage or tenement called Freron Lodge [later Manor Farm now the North Middlesex Golf Club] with appurtenances in the parish of Friern Barnet, late of Dame Ellen Proby, and that other Capital messuage or Manor House [now Friary

Park] and the manor called Whetstone lying in the parish of Friern Barnet and all other messuages, cottages and lands in the possession of the Manor.

Even by 1811, Whetstone was still described as "a straggling village of mean cottages and inns."

SOME EARLY HOUSES

The junction of what became Athenaeum Road and the High Road was described as the north end of Whetstone Town in 1500, giving a good idea of the size of the village at that time. The oldest remnants of a house in the district are probably at 1266 High Road, now the offices of Pilgrim, the property company. This was owned by the Ffoxe family of Bowes in 1484 and some of the original timber and wattle and daub survive in the attic. The family also owned land in Southgate, hence Fox Lane. In 1613 the property was described as "a messuage, stable and garden called the Fox inn"; by 1662 it had become The Crown and by 1849 it was divided between a bakery and a boot repair shop.

No. 1264, sometimes wrongly said to be the oldest house in the borough, has a mixed history. In the fifteenth century it was owned by the

144. *The High Road, Whetstone, in 1863. On the left can be seen the Green Man pub sign.*

145. *The High Road, Whetstone c.1860. The couple on the right are sitting on the old stone, which originally stood much closer to the pub. It was moved in 1863. The Gilmour sisters are in the doorway of their shop.*

146. The High Road, Whetstone, c.1905. The Griffin Inn is to the right.

147. The demolition of the turnpike gate at the High Road, Whetstone in October 1863. The clock and the board listing the toll changes can be seen on the wall of the toll keeper's house.

148. The High Road, Whetstone, c.1912. Smith's Cottages in the centre of the picture were demolished in the 1930s and replaced by the Westminster Bank.

Sanny family – in 1552 John Sanny left money to mend "the road from Taterygge to Wheston called Braynt Lane" (now Totteridge Lane). The house grew into two properties, one a bakery, and another an alehouse called The Griffin (first mentioned by name in 1694 and rebuilt 1929). Another house was put up at the rear of the site, described in 1549 as "lately built". All three were purchased in 1739 by Richard Brown. The Griffin was sold to Meux the brewers in 1837, and soon afterwards the original house was joined to the one at the rear by a draper called Robert Parker. His partner, Robert Gilmour, also operated the toll gate which stood outside The Griffin, exactly where the traffic lights are today. When the gate was abolished Gilmour took over the post office which he installed inside the draper's shop. At his death his daughters managed the post office and it was said that no postcard was ever delivered in Whetstone or Totteridge until they had read it first.

After the last war part of the shop was used by Studio Cole as a photographic business, but the building was sadly neglected until 1998 when it was taken over by Pizza Express. It was then thoroughly refurbished.

Two other old houses in the High Road remain. These are The Limes at no.1333, where a drainpipe has the initials of Richard Bridgemour and his wife Elizabeth, and Ivy House at no.1331. The latter was described in 1683 as "partly brick and partly timber with a garden, a brew house and a carpenter's shop. By 1810 it was owned by Thomas Dixon who was the landlord of Peter Mountain, stage coach proprietor, who had stables next door. The stables were replaced by Solomon's Terrace which in turn was replaced by the Waitrose store.

CHURCH PATH

The extent of modern-day Whetstone is generally thought to be between Woodside Lane in the south, Walfield Avenue in the north and the Dollis Brook in the west.

Just north of Woodside Lane, the Swan Lane recreation ground was once used as a source of gravel to make up the High Road.

149. The Newton cycle shop in St John's Row, Whetstone c.1910. The Newton family later branched out into motor cars and eventually owned a large garage at the foot of Barnet Hill.

Church Path now runs from Swan Lane to North Finchley, but it is only part of an ancient route, probably 600 years old, leading from Whetstone to Finchley parish church. It originally ran straight to the main Whetstone cross roads but was turned by the Woodside estate at Swan Lane.

Swan Lane is named from another Swan with Two Necks pub (*see p104*) which was opened in 1728. A return of 1756 shows that it had two beds and seven stables available. In the 1840s it was bought by Robert Lloyd who had been a driver on the London-Birmingham coaches. It was pulled down in 1980 and replaced by a block of flats, South Mount and North Mount.

MAKING FILMS

The site of a house called Coldharbour, on the east side of the High Road just north of Woodside Lane, and first mentioned in 1614, is now occupied by E.M.C. and Mills Shopfitting. It was originally called Hopkins, perhaps after a former owner. He built a second house on half an acre immediately to the south which became a pub called the Spotted Dog, described in 1701 as "a house and large garden with stables and a brew house". In 1822 John Bacon owned "Those two messuages, formerly one, known as the 'Dog' and afterwards the 'Queens Head', lately converted to two private houses with barns and stables". It had stabling for 45 horses and was used in 1790 by John Kendrick a horse dealer. The houses were bought by Frederick Shenton, an architect who renovated them in 1886. One of these houses is now called Derwent House and the second, Woodlands, was used by British Empire Films from 1913 until 1923 and by British Famous Films from 1923 to 1930. There was an open sided film

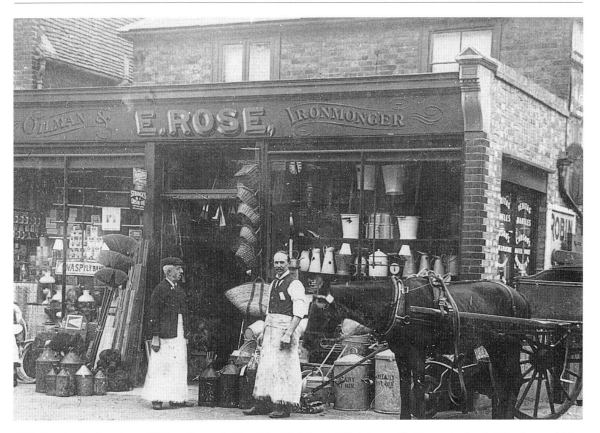

150. Rose's oil shop at no. 1325 on the west side of the High Road, Whetstone. Mr Rose is in front of the door and his son-in-law, a Mr Oliver, is to his left.

set so that natural light could be used for filming. In addition they had 250 volt DC lighting.

The studio perforated, developed and printed its own films in a basement laboratory and the building also had dressing rooms and offices. They specialised in bringing plays from the West End stage and filming them, sometimes using a large lake – now part of North Middlesex golf course – for naval scenes.

A local resident, Jack Prime, gave a description of how the studio recruited local school children to play minor parts in 1915.

> One Saturday about twenty of us were asked to go there for a school scene. The story was about a sailor coming home on leave. He comes to school and scrambles a handful of pennies. We were allowed to keep what we got. We had biscuits, ham sandwiches and lemonade for lunch and I remember that we sat with the star and thought how pretty she was. We also asked her how she made up her eyes and she told us … it was done with a hairpin held in the flame

of a candle and then applied to the top and bottom eye lids. At the end of the day we were given sixpence each.

The studio closed because they could not afford the equipment needed to make talkies.

Woodlands was given its name in 1891 by John Salmon who lived there, while it was being used as a studio, until his death in 1923. In 1938 it was described as "Up 3 beds front, long passage to servants' quarters, 2 beds back. Servants 2 beds, attic, 1 long room". From 1947 until 1951 the premises were used as a restaurant.

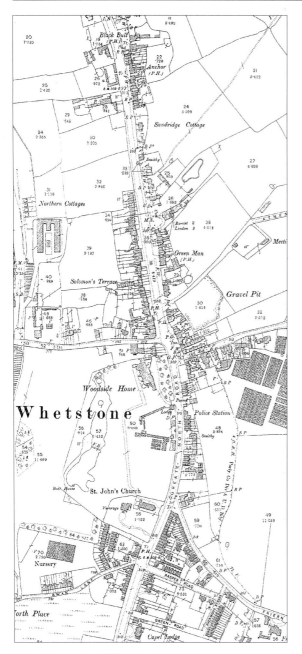

151. *The centre of Whetstone in 1897.*

152. *A storage cistern at the rear wall of no. 1264 High Road, Whetstone, photographed in 1989 during an archaeological excavation.*

153. *A north wall on the first floor of the same building, with mullioned window and wind brace.*

154. The old stone outside the Griffin Inn at Whetstone, made of quartz and sandstone. This may have been the base of a fair cross, and it was certainly used as a horse mounting block.

155. Mills shopfitting in the High Road, Whetstone, occupies part of the old Coldharbour complex of buildings (see p.110)

156. Joseph Baxendale.

THE MARTYN LANDS

The Martyn lands were between what is now Swan Lane and Totteridge Lane, and from the High Road west to Dollis Brook. These became the Woodside estate (1773) and included Wood End Field and Woods Corner Field. They may well have belonged to Adam de Basing in 1254, but they did belong to the Martyn family from 1308 until 1489. John Martyn died in 1487 leaving them to his daughter Olive. In 1471, the year of the Battle of Barnet – one of the more important of the conflicts in the Wars of the Roses – John Martyn was charged with non-payment of tithes. In 1488 Agnes Martyn left money in her will to "keep open for ever the path from Fayre Cross at Whetstone to the Parish Church of St Mary at Finchley" (now Church Path and Nether Street).

A will of about 1680 refers to the 'King's Arms' on the Martyn lands.

Joseph Baxendale (1785-1872) bought the Woodside estate in 1824.

He was born in Lancaster, worked in the calico business and soon made enough money to buy up the ailing transport firm of Pickford Brothers. His superb organisational skills resulted in a regular and punctual network involving canals and horse transport. He saw the potential of railways early and was a major shareholder in

157. *The library at the Baxendale house, c.1870.*

the London, South East & Folkestone Railway and in the Paris Nord railway company. He bought Folkestone harbour and in 1851 suggested linking his two railways by driving a tunnel under the English Channel.

The 1881 census shows Joseph Baxendale, his wife Mary and daughter Jane, with a butler, two footmen, a cook, a kitchen maid, two house maids, two lady's maids, a hand maid and a secretary all living in the house.

In 1882 there was a cricket match when his gardeners played his grooms using his lawn as the cricket ground.

After his retirement he was chairman of the local bench of magistrates and also Deputy Lieutenant of the county. Whenever there was a collection for local charities, his name was at the top of the list of subscribers. His name is commemorated in a road just south of Totteridge Lane called, simply, Baxendale

His house was the first in the district to be lit by gas, which was stored in a holder at the foot of Totteridge Lane just past the brook until it was demolished about 1870 because it was feared that it might be a target for Fenians.

ST JOHN'S CHURCH AND SCHOOL

In 1832 Baxendale gave part of his garden to build St John's church, which was consecrated on 9 May that year. The architect for what was originally a rather plain church may possibly have been the Bishop of London himself, Charles Blomfield, renowned for the energy with which he pushed through a major church building programme in London. Improvements were made in 1879 by James Brooks, and the east window is from the studio of William Morris.

St John's School was opened about 1839 in a disused building in Totteridge Lane which had previously been the parish poor house – the parish priest, the Revd Henry Ventris, was the first teacher. A new school was opened in Britannia Road, on the other side of the High Road, in 1863.

There were many complaints about unruly behaviour. In 1875 "the school children are very backward and unruly" wrote one teacher. Another said "The children are very backward and disorderly. I have addressed them on their behaviour." In 1882 (and then for 34 years) the head teacher was Mr B. Mellor, of a family associated with local schools for over fifty years.

ARCHERY PRACTICE

The Three Horse Shoes (*ill. 161*) was built about 1880, on the south junction of Friern Barnet Lane and the High Road, on the site of an earlier pub, which had been operated by William Bass, a farrier. The Esso garage stands on the site of the archery butts where up to Tudor times all men were required to practise archery in case of a need to defend the realm. Obviously such a dangerous sport could only be conducted on waste land and the triangle formed when the main highway north moved from Friern Barnet Lane to the High Road through Finchley created just such a space at the junction of those roads, just north of today's Friern Barnet Lane. The space remained open

158. St John's Church, Whetstone c.1905.

159. A class at St John's Infants' School, pre 1914.

160. Copps Dairy in Friern Barnet Lane, in the 1920s. The Copps and the Floyd family were related by marriage. The cows were grazed near Russell Lane and were walked along Oakleigh Road and Whetstone High Road twice daily to be milked. The dairy was taken over by the United Dairies. The site is now Whetstone Police Station.

until 1748 when Thomas Hunt opened a blacksmith's forge there.

Round the corner in Friern Barnet Lane was Copp's dairy, the site of which is now taken by a police station. The Home Secretary ordered in 1818 that three men of each patrol should live at the outward extremity of their beat and patrol inwards. The first police station was built in March 1862. The old station was pulled down in the 1970s and replaced by an office block now occupied by M. Berman & Co.

The Whetstone fire station (*ill. 163*) immediately to the north was a wooden hut used to store a hand pump, hose carts and ladders. The Howard brothers, who were local builders, were part-time firemen and looked after the equipment.

The Hand and Flower pub (*ill. 162*) on the corner of the High Road and Oakleigh Road was also known as the Black Horse or White Horse. It is recorded in 1609 as a tenement with three acres, and by 1741 it was three tenements, formerly two, "together with a well of water and a piece of ground, formerly waste, fronting the turnpike road abutting west on a pond lying on the common".

The building was reconstructed in 1905 with ornate plasterwork, but pulled down in 1990. It is now a Barclay's bank.

BOMBING PRACTICE

Whetstone Place, just south of Swan Lane in the High Road, was built as Lynn's Rents about 1840. No. 1 was the local tax office occupied by Joseph Hawkins (*see ill.164*), who collected the rates as well as excise duties. In such bad condition were the properties that in 1939 they were offered to Finchley Council for a Civil Defence exercise. A Blenheim bomber flew over the High Road in a simulated bombing run. The two end houses were used to practise rescue from a collapsed building and the rest of the terrace was to be used for fire fighting (*ill. 165*). Unfortunately the houses would not catch fire at first, but eventually produced enough smoke to block the High Road. The site is now taken by Swan Court.

On the other side of the High Road, Portland Terrace in Rasper Road is dated 1870. St John's Terrace opposite the church was built by Miss Berger about 1880. Miss Berger lived with her sister in Friern House in Friern Barnet Lane. They owned the cottages nearby and Brook Farm further along the High Road. On 6 October 1884, Miss Berger, while trying to rescue a boy, was badly gored by a bull. She was rescued by farm men,

161. *The Three Horse Shoes, Friern Barnet Lane, painted about 1890, at which time the landlords were the Copps family.*

162. *The Hand and Flower on the south side of Whetstone crossroads, about 1905. Earlier names included the White Horse and the Black Horse. It was replaced by Barclays Bank.*

163. The old Whetstone fire station. This housed a hand pump, hose carts, ladders and tools. The station was supervised by the Howard brothers, local builders.

but was so seriously injured that she spent the rest of her life in a wheel chair.

Swan Place was an alley of twelve small cottages opposite the end of Swan Lane, in which no. 8 was the Whetstone School of Cookery. During the bad winters of the 1880s and '90s this served as a soup kitchen for the local poor paid for by the Baxendales. Pulled down in 1939, it is now a branch of the Anglo Irish bank.

MR SWEET'S NURSERY

About 1865 William Davies opened a small nursery in Oakleigh Road which he subsequently sold to James Sweet. Sweet had served his apprenticeship in two large houses in Stanmore. He then worked at a large commercial nursery in Chelmsford before moving to Whetstone in 1884 where he enlarged the grounds and built himself a house called White Lodge. He specialised in hot house plants and heather which he exported *to* Scotland and every night he sent a cart full of flowers to Covent Garden market.

164. Joseph Hawkins, tax collector, outside Lynn's Rents, which were built about 1840. These premises were later used for fire fighting and rescue from bombed buildings (see p.117).

165. Whetstone Place was set alight on 20 May 1939 in order to practise wartime fire-fighting techniques.

In 1902 he received an emergency call from the Royal Horticultural Society. A train carrying flowers for the Chelsea Flower Show had broken down and they were short of exhibits and so he diverted his usual delivery to Chelsea. He was later made a Fellow of the Royal Horticultural Society and in 1920 awarded its Victoria Medal of Honour.

He retired from the business in 1913 when he was succeeded by his sons Graham, Arthur and Lionel.

Although he worshipped at St John's Whetstone he was very friendly with Father Miles and so, after his death on 7 June 1924, he was buried at St James' Friern Barnet.

During the last war the nursery was requisitioned for use as an anti-aircraft gun site imaginatively named Glasshouses and later it housed army records until 1969. It was bought by Friern Barnet Council and used for houses for rent known as Sweets Way.

TOTTERIDGE LANE

The row of shops between the Bull and Butcher and Totteridge Lane were demolished in 2001. It is likely that this strip of land had been occupied for over 600 years. The early records are lost but in 1804 William Chambers bought "that piece of land lying north of Totteridge Lane". In 1829 it was sold by James Saunders, baker, to another baker and eventually to James Harper who had a baker's business in Hadley. The Harper family were to run the bakery for over 100 years. When the shops were rebuilt about 1880, all traces of the earlier properties were destroyed by the new cellars.

Further down Totteridge Lane, about where Waitrose's car park comes out, was The George, described in 1596 as "my house in Whetstone with the little backhouse, also a little house called The Cliphouse". About 1680 the pub was closed down and its licensee moved to Finchley where he opened another pub of the same name together with a pig market (*see p43*).

Thomas Newman owned Whetstone House in 1826 and Francis Newman is shown in 1892. It was demolished about 1930 and replaced by Station Parade.

Totteridge Station was opened in 1872 on the Great Northern Railway. There were extensive coal sidings, now used as a car park, and the nearby stables and horse hospital included a special sweating room similar to the one owned at Woodside by Baxendale. The theory was that by putting the horses in a very hot, metal lined room they would sweat out any illness.

The Bull and Butcher (*ill. 168*) is on a site first

166. *Excavation at the corner of Totteridge Lane and High Road in 2001. Most of the early material had been destroyed when cellars were dug in the 1880s. Walls from Georgian cottages and a small amount of pottery from the 14th century and later were found.*

167. *Harper's bakery on the corner of High Road and Totteridge Lane in c.1880, a building pulled down about 1881. The family continued to run the shop until 1939, when it became Hillside Bakeries.*

168. The Bull and Butcher in Whetstone High Road, before the arrival of the trams in 1906. James Solomon, known as 'King' Solomon, stands proudly in front of the pub which he owned. He also built the nearby Solomon's Terrace.

mentioned on 9 October 1375. In 1406, John Haybourne complained in the manorial court that his tenant Isabella Wyrhales had left to waste the hall, barns and tenement which she held. Other names for the pub since have included the Princes Arms and in 1675 the Black Lion. It was rebuilt in its present form in 1928.

THE ATTFIELD HOUSE

At the corner of High Road and Oakleigh Road North in 1486 John Doggett owned a cottage "with curtilage and three crofts called Beldam, Middlefield and Cokkefield". By 1796 Richard Attfield had replaced the cottage by three cottages running east down Oakleigh Road. Attfield, who came to Whetstone in 1790, was a grocer and a parish clerk. He had beautiful handwriting. It is in his hand that a moving entry in the parish accounts reads: "To burying a poor unknown boy 6d, and a box for putting him in 4d.

Attfield planted a row of elm trees along the High Road which were a feature that the Whetstone Society today seeks to emulate. The cottages were demolished after 1881 and the present row of yellow brick shops erected.

Attfield's grandson was Professor John Attfield, born in the family home in 1835. He was edu-

169. Professor John Attfield.

cated at Queen Elizabeth's School in Barnet and apprenticed to the Pharmaceutical Society for three years. He scored full marks in every examination paper and won first prize in every subject in his final year 1853/4. He was Professor of Practical Chemistry for the Society from 1862 until 1896 and was largely responsible for the acceptance of the sign BP as a complete guarantee of drug purity. His standard work *Chemistry – General, Medical and Pharmaceutical* ran to 19 editions and was for more than a century the pharmacist's bible. He died in Watford in 1911.

AROUND THE GREEN MAN
The Green Man is one of Whetstone's oldest pubs, which may have belonged to the Heybourne family as early as 1400. It was called the Lion in 1485, when John Doggett sold it to Thomas Copewood. It was a droving inn, with fields at the rear and a large pond. It was rebuilt about 1740, refronted in 1830 and again in 1891. The former stables are now the Green Man garage.

THE OAKLEIGH PARK ESTATE
This estate is laid out on land bought in 1820 by Sir Simon Haughton Clarke, said to have been the seventh richest man in England. He lived at Oakhill House in East Barnet. Some of the land was bought by the Whetstone Freehold Estate Co.

in 1869 and the first seven houses in Oakleigh Park North – from the Hollies to The Acorns and Beaufront – had been built by 1871. Oakleigh Park South was partly built by 1881 – in 1874 the *Barnet Press* had been advertising building plots for houses of not less than £1,000. Development was speeded up by the opening of Oakleigh Park station in 1873.

The Lodge, 13 Oakleigh Park North, was used by the Soviet newsagency Tass as a cover for spying activities based on radio intercepts at the height of the Cold War. In particular they were bugging the RAF network covering the defence of London. This espionage was discovered, the staff were declared *persona non grata* and the station was closed.

Many of the rich residents of this area were nonconformists who paid to have a church built on the corner between Oakleigh Park North and Oakleigh Road North. This affluence also resulted in friction between the East Barnet and the Colney Hatch gas companies as to which of them should supply this lucrative area (*ills 171 & 172*).

The northernmost houses in Myddelton Park (1880) and All Saints' church on the corner with Oakleigh Road North were built with the aid of the philanthropic John Miles (*see p.125*). The architect of the church was J. Clarke. The All Saints Girls' School (*ill. 175*) was opened adjacent in 1889, but this closed in 1969 and the buildings are now used as a youth club.

170. The Green Man, about 1912. The fields at the rear, amounting to some 8 acres, were used by drovers for grazing cattle on their way to Smithfield Market.

172. *The gasholder of the Colney Hatrch Gas, Light and Coke company at New Southgate. The company was incorporated in 1858 but not fully functional until 1866.*

171. *A reminder of the battle between gas companies to supply the affluent Oakleigh Park Estate - a boundary mark in Oakleigh Park North to denote the territories of the East Barnet and Colney Hatch gas companies. (Photo 1991)*

Sir Charles Groves, the conductor, (1915-92) lived in Queens Avenue and sang in the choir at All Saints. He studied at the Royal College of Music (1932-7), was appointed chorus master to the BBC (1938) and became successively assistant conductor to the BBC Theatre Orchestra, the BBC Northern Orchestra and the Bournemouth Symphony Orchestra. He was with the Royal Liverpool Philharmonic from 1963-77, and was also conductor for English National Opera and the Welsh National Opera. He specialised in the music of Mahler and Maxwell Davies.

Oakleigh Infants' School was the first state school in the district. It was opened in 1928 at 116 Oakleigh Road North and was much overcrowded – by 1931 the head teacher had a class of 55 and a newly-made class of 58 was being taught by a young teacher straight from college. The opening of Queenswell school and the new Catholic school in Oakleigh Park made the buildings redundant and they were reopened as All Saints Church of England School in 1969.

Early council housing appeared in Oakleigh Road North when, in 1920, Friern Barnet council issued a compulsory purchase order for land there for the sum of £7,200. 45 houses were erected for £30,805. There was another order for Morley's Farm in 1921, the site of which was covered by Miles Way, Barfield Avenue and Simmons Way, all named after local personalities.

THE ATHENAEUM
Athenaeum Road recalls the Athenaeum Club, formed in 1881 by George Waterlow, of Beaufront, Oakleigh Park, for residents interested in literature, science and the arts. (The Waterlow family owned a well-known City printers specialising in bank notes.) In 1881 the accommodation in his club, converted from barns, included a hall seating 400 persons, a billiard room, a library and a kitchen with a good coal range. It opened on 11 March 1881 with a grand concert ('Carriages at 10.30'), together with other entertainments which included a drill display by the NCOs of the Royal Fusiliers, a gymnastic display and pantomimes. A recital planned for February 1885 was cancelled for lack of support, and in August George Waterlow moved to Harrow. In 1886 the building was a dry plate photographic works and by the 1920s it was used by Direct Dry Cleaners. The site is now covered by Oxford Gardens.

173. All Saints church in Oakleigh Road, about 1920.

174. Father Henry Miles, vicar of All Saints.

THE BUCKINGHAM/CHANDOS AVENUE ESTATE

These were open fields, known in 1790 as Hemmings Lands. James Brydges, (1674-1744) Duke of Chandos and Marquis of Buckingham, was paymaster-general from 1705-14, and also the recipient of a contract to supply hay to the army about 1715. In order to do this he bought up large tracts of land in an arc around north London running from Edgware, through Hendon, Mill Hill, Totteridge, Barnet and Enfield. He turned all this land over to grass and made enormous profits. In a large house called Canons he built near Edgware he employed Handel as music master, together with his own professional orchestra and choir, for whom Handel wrote the Chandos Anthems.

When Chandos bought the Hemmings Lands they consisted of Pond Field (5 acres), Little Field (2), Further field (3), First English Field (3), Further English Field (3), Cuckolds (2) and some other closes; descendants added the Grange estate at the top of today's Chandos Avenue in 1820.

The whole estate was sold for development in 1892. Chandos Avenue, from Oakleigh Park Station towards Whetstone, was completely built

175. *Architect's drawing of All Saints Girls' School in Oakleigh Road. Now used as a youth club.*

176. *Chandos Avenue c.1930.*

177. The Sailor's Home Refreshment Rooms next to the Black Bull in Whetstone c.1920.

up by 1926. In the same year Langton Avenue had only two houses, nos. 2 & 4, while Buckingham Avenue was being laid out in plots. Friern Mount Drive and Temple Avenue had been settled by 1935. Franklin Close (c.1970) was named after a former town clerk of Finchley.

Archbishops Temple and Langton, though commemorated in road names, have no link with the district.

The Black Bull pub in the High Road, just south of Buckingham Avenue, was in existence in 1750 when the licensee was Jonathan Cooper, and by 1880 it belonged to Thomas Moulton, who also farmed the fields opposite. The dance hall at the rear was used in the 1920s as a training facility by many boxers including Len Harvey.

An item in the *Barnet Press* of 20 August 1887, refers to a resident in the High Road, near the Black Bull:

> Interesting case of longevity, Mrs Mary O'Briern a centenarian who has lived in Whetstone for over 40 years, reached her 105th birthday last Lady Day. Her husband was an employee of Messrs Bracey, and she had a pension of 8 shillings per week. He was employed on the construction of the GNR and was killed when the tunnel collapsed. Mrs O'Briern also has 3s 6d per week from the parish and her rent is 1s 6d. She has the use of her facilities, but her eyesight in no longer good enough for work and her hearing is defective. She is living in the house of Mr Gorrett in the High Road.

The East Barnet Gas and Water Company began laying water mains along Whetstone High Road on 11 Sept. 1869, resulting in the following property advertisement in the *Barnet Press*:

> It is hoped that property owners will avail themselves of the opportunity. It is a good investment, because cottages without fever etc. and with clean water will let for substantially higher rents.

However not all houses had taps fitted and wells continued in use until about 1915.

The Grange, in the High Road, was traditionally the home of the Whetstone doctor throughout the nineteenth century. It had been turned into a private asylum by 1900 but was developed into a large private residence by William Jelks, the furniture store owner, by 1926.

WALFIELD

The northernmost estate in Whetstone or Friern Barnet was Walfield. Traditionally it was occupied by the manor bailiff, perhaps to keep an eye on possible encroachments at the county boundary. In 1486, John Pratt, the bailiff, on his deathbed surrendered "the messuage in which he lived – two small cottages and a croft of land containing 3 acres called Walfield", to John Pratt his son, also "two crofts which lie at Colney Hatch called Newmans also the other called Collip".

On 26 August 1796 "Henry William Lauzan was admitted to Walfield and a new messuage erected." This is shown in 1814-5 as a house and forecourt together with a close called Cockfield. By 1844 it was occupied by Ann Lauzan. In 1798, Henry Lauzan and his partners bought out the business of Jacob Schweppe, the inventor of the well known artificial mineral water.

The 1851 census shows Charles Brewerton aged 46, a house proprietor living at Walfield, renting it from Miss Lauzan. The *Barnet Press* of 30 October 1884 has an advertisement for the sale by auction of Walfield, the property of the late Charles Brewerton, and the Friern Barnet rate book for 1898 shows the house and garden of four acres owned by A. Berry and occupied by Helene Pfotzer, and nearby Whetstone House owned and occupied by S. Grocott. Whetstone House appears to date from about 1800.

Walfield was demolished in 1964 and replaced by Farnham Close. The nearby Walfield Avenue commemorates the name but is on the wrong side of the main road. Whetstone House (not to be confused with Whetstone House in Totteridge Lane) was demolished about 1987 and replaced by a block of flats called Walfield House.

THE WHETSTONE SOCIETY

In modern times the Whetstone Society has been formed to preserve the amenities of the area. One strand of it began when a group of shopkeepers got together to preserve the buildings on the corner of Totteridge Lane and the High Road, but unfortunately English Heritage did not think them worthy of listing. Opposition to redevelopment continued until 1999 when permission to develop was given.

In 1989 the Society amalgamated with the Whetstone Residents' Association which had been opposing the B & Q development, to form the Whetstone Society. The Society spearheaded the campaign to refurbish 1264 High Road (formerly Studio Cole and now Pizza Express), and as a result the first ever compulsory repair notice was issued by the council and the building was upgraded to Grade II*. Other issues the Society has been concerned with are the retention of Whetstone Stray opposite Totteridge station, and the planting of trees in the locality.

178. Walfield in the High Road. Dating from c.1780, it was demolished in 1964. Its site is now taken by Farnham Close.1780.

Totteridge

Diana Griffith's splendid *Book of Totteridge* is still available and this section is intended to complement rather than repeat what she has written.

Totteridge is probably a corruption of Tata's Ridge. Tata is a Saxon personal name, which also occurs in Tatta Burn, now Folly Brook.

A recently discovered charter dating from about 1005 describing the boundaries of Barnet includes a reference to the boundary with Totteridge. It is reasonable to assume therefore that there were people living in Totteridge a thousand years ago. Other forms of the name include Taterigg, Tateryche and Teterig.

The boundaries of Totteridge are largely natural. They run from Dollis Brook on the north and west, to Folly Brook on the south and what was described as Totteridge marsh, lying near Highwood Hill.

Because the soil of the area was wet, heavy clay, the vegetation would have included oak, elm and willow in the valleys. Blackberries, hawthorn, stinging nettles and coarse grass and, more attractively, flowers like primroses, cowslips, foxgloves and honeysuckle would have colonised the clearings.

The place is not mentioned by name in the Domesday Survey. It was the property of the Bishop of Ely as part of the manor of Hatfield, given to the abbot by Edward the Confessor, and is probably included with Hatfield.

Totteridge has always been small – the total acreage is 1,604. The Inquisition of 1257 shows 293 acres under profitable cultivation, 7° mown and 13 of grove sown with acorns and nuts. In 1277 a survey recorded a population which included 12 tenants and 27 copyholders, together with a church and a windmill. By about 1350 there was "a great hall, chapel and separate chambers for knights, esquires and clerks".

The Land Tax assessment of 1524 has 12 land owners or lease holders, and seven farms valued at £3 or more. The list for 1545 has 17 land occupiers.

Writing in 1796, Lysons says "The present number of houses is 58 – 14 mansions, 8 farm houses, 4 tradesmen, 2 public houses and 30 cottages".

The Bishop was the lord of the manor until 1562 when it was passed to Queen Elizabeth in exchange for a pension to the Bishop. Later lords included the Duke of Chandos (*see p125*) in 1721 and the Lee family. Sir Albert Barratt, who lived at Totteridge Park, was lord in 1934. S.G. Barratt

179. St Andrew's, Totteridge, c.1905.

published a well researched history of Totteridge, no doubt financed by the success of his famous liquorice allsorts.

There has been a church at Totteridge since at least 1250 and the yew tree in the churchyard is said to be over 900 years old. There is an early engraving of St Andrew's suggesting a seventeenth-century building with wooden casement windows. A wooden tower was added in 1702 but the church was rebuilt in 1790. The west porch was built in 1845 and there were further alterations in 1869; the north vestry was added in 1897. The pulpit was brought from the mother church of St Etheldreda at Hatfield – indeed, the dedication to St Andrew may be a corruption of St Etheldreda.

Early tax returns contain names like Colyer and Colieres, implying the presence of charcoal burners. Charcoal was used for heating and for absorbing the smells caused by poor drainage and sanitation.

In Norman times perhaps as many as six families may have lived in the parish, eking out a meagre living in the woods. They would have kept a few pigs to supply meat and leather and probably sheep and goats for milk and hides.

Goats do not like the wet so they would have needed some kind of shelter. The trees were gradually cut down to provide timber for buildings and fences but also to provide firewood for cooking. The grazing animals would have eaten sprouting trees and bushes so regeneration was stopped and the amount of grass gradually increased. Because the soil was so difficult to work the predominant crop was grass.

There is a grant dated 1251 giving the Bishop of Ely 'free right of warren'. Because rabbits eat grass it is reasonable to assume that there were enough open fields to make it worthwhile.

'The Priory' is a group of much restored Jacobean cottages. They were bought by a Mrs Garrow, whose relatives lived in the 'Priory' at Hadley. She had been so happy with them that she named her house after theirs.

The tithe barn dates from the seventeenth century. The nearby pound is a reminder of the value of grass as a cash crop. Beasts found straying and eating unauthorised grass were impounded and not released until a fee had been paid. The nearby Pound House was designed by J.L. Williams and built in 1907.

180. *The Priory at Totteridge, basically a group of restored Jacobean cottages.*

181. Copped Hall, Totteridge, c.1905.

THE COPPED HALL

The Copped Hall is now vanished but formerly stood opposite the church. It may have got its name from the shape of its roof – a copped, peaked or high gabled roof. It was the home of Edward Cliffe until his death in 1632. In 1796 it was bought by William Manning, a director of the Bank of England, whose son, Henry Edward, became a Roman Catholic bishop in 1865 and a cardinal in 1893. He died in 1903 and is buried in the crypt of Westminster Cathedral.

Sir Samuel Boulton (1830-1918) bought Copped Hall in 1894. He invited Cardinal Manning to revisit the house where Manning had been born and they became good friends. Boulton, who was lord of the manor and chairman of the Barnet bench, was also a founder of the London Labour Conciliation Board which helped settle numerous industrial dispute in the 1880s and 1890s. He always acknowledged the help that Cardinal Manning had given him at that time. For some fifty years, Boulton was chairman of the Dominion Tar & Chemical Company and was very active in promoting the use of scientific methods in industry. He wrote many pamphlets and newspaper articles on social, economic and industrial subjects.

Copped Hall was demolished in 1929 and replaced by 'Darlands' built for George Herbert Kemp, one of Totteridge's most important ben-efactors, who made his fortune in biscuits and was the last lord of the manor. He died in 1942. The new house was designed by Sir E. Guy Dawber (1861-1938). It had six reception rooms, eight bedrooms, four bathrooms, a staff cottage and a four-car garage. Dawber was a founder member of the Society for the Preservation of Rural England and worked extensively in the Cotswolds.

In 1965 Barnet Council bought 72 acres of agricultural land behind Darlands as Green Belt land for the sum of £43,000. At the same auction the house was sold in less than five minutes for £53,000, though the council had already bought the lake and boat house. The whole site is now a nature reserve.

THE VICARAGE

The vicarage next to the church is the first work of Sir Charles Nicholson the architect in 1892 (*see below*). A map of 1790 shows a parsonage on roughly the present site. In 1638 and 1693, the curate's house in Totteridge had "one orchard garden with a little Backside contayning by estimacion 2 roods, and 7½ acres of pasture land".

The Revd Abel Lendon was perpetual curate of Totteridge from 1814 to 1842. and at much the same time he was Rector of Friern Barnet as well, possibly because the populations of both parishes were so small that the duties were fairly light.

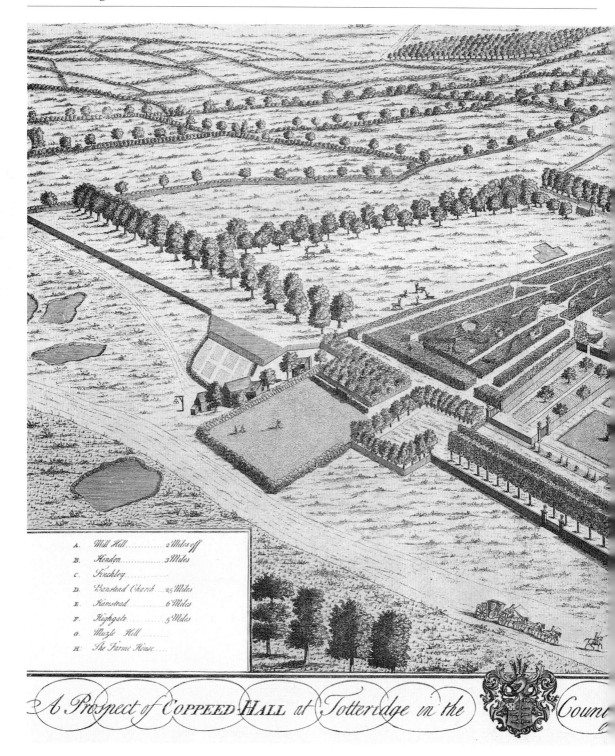

A.	Mill Hill	2 Miles off
B.	Hendon	3 Miles
C.	Finchley	
D.	Banstead Church	2,5 Miles
E.	Hamstead	6 Miles
F.	Highgate	5 Miles
G.	Muzle Hill	
H.	The Farme House	

A Prospect of COPPEED HALL *at* Totteridge *in the* Count

182.   *A panoramic view of Copped Hall, Totteridge, the seat of Joseph da Costa, looking south c.1725. The hills of Highgate and Hampstead can be seen in the left far distance.*

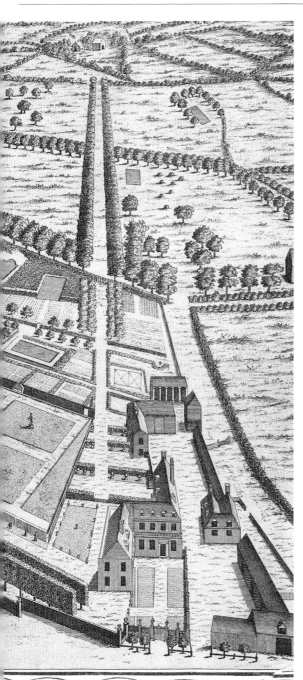

FORD the Seat of Joseph da Costa

He lived at Wykeham Rise but at one time appears to have owned both Rose Hill and Holme Lodge. He ran a school at Wykeham Rise where his pupils in 1920s included the future Cardinal Manning.

Garden Hill, formerly Rose Hill, opposite the church, was the home of the Marsham family in the 1840s. It is a classic example of Georgian architecture dating from about 1750. In the 1930s it was the home of Lord Hewart, the Lord Chief Justice who had a special, personal delivery of mail every morning. The stable block on the north side was converted in to a house in the 1990s.

Southernhay, also opposite the church and sometimes known as Holme Lodge, was inspected by R.E. Cowley in the late 1950s. He reported seeing Tudor bricks in the cellar walls and considers it to be the site of the original manor house for Totteridge. It would certainly be appropriate for the manor house to be near the church. The present building seems to date from the early 1800s.

THE NICHOLSONS

The Grange in Totteridge Lane was burned down on 22 February 1899 but was rebuilt on the existing ground plan and in a very similar style to its 1787 predecessor.

The Nicholsons, arguably the most talented family to have lived at Totteridge, resided at The Grange from 1875. Sir Charles Nicholson (1808-1903), had a string of university degrees. He trained as a physician in Edinburgh and later emigrated to his uncle's property in New South Wales where he was eventually to become the first Speaker of the Assembly and chancellor of the local university. At the time he bought The Grange from Frederick Wood the boundary with the neighbouring Manor Farm House was confused. He straightened it out in both senses and had a stable block built. He amassed a large collection of Etruscan, Roman and Greek antiquities.

His elder son Charles (1867-1949) was an architect and won the Tite prize in 1893. He was consulting architect to seven cathedrals and his local work included rebuilding The Grange after the fire and designing Totteridge vicarage. In 1907 he designed the King's House and government buildings in Kingston, Jamaica using reinforced concrete after the earthquake that year, probably the first use of concrete on such a scale.

The second son, Sir Sydney Nicholson (1875-1947), was organist at Barnet parish church in

1897. In 1908 he became organist and choir master at Manchester Cathedral. He built up the choir to such a high standard that he was promoted to Westminster Abbey in 1918, where his annual performances of Bach's *St Matthew Passion* became renowned. He left the Abbey in 1927 in order to spend more time on church music and in 1928 founded the (Royal) School of Church Music. He also edited *Hymns Ancient and Modern* and was a gifted amateur painter.

Archibald Nicholson, a third son, was a designer of stained glass with his own studio in St John's Wood.

In December 1933 The Grange and its grounds were bought by Frank Parvin, who converted the house into flats and laid out Grange Avenue where he lived himself.

GRAND HOUSES

What is now called the Manor House on Totteridge Common was originally Totteridge Manor Farm house. It was refronted for John Fiott in 1793.

Totteridge Park further east is another strong candidate for the site of the original manor house (*see Southernhay above*). The present building is dated 1750 and may well be on the site of an earlier house. The estate encompassed about 100 acres. The Arrowsmiths rented the house about 1811. Louisa Arrowsmith kept a detailed dairy. She records:

> 1818 September 26
> The two watchmen Thomas Stanley and Jeremiah Seagrave began their watch. They caught a man named McCarthy who was with another stripping the copper off Mr Hunter's summer house. They were hammering it in Mr Hall's field to put it in a sack. They secured McCarthy, who strongly resisted so much as to endanger the life of Thomas Stanley. They bound him and tied his hands and brought him to the Park at 3 o'clock where they secured him in a stable until 6 o'clock when they took him to the Orange Tree and lodg'd him with the Constable.

The watch was less successful in 1830. It was reported that:

> Four robberies committed in the village. Mr Osmond's, the Church, The Orange Tree and the Blacksmith's shop. They took all the books out of the pews, many of them being left in Barnet Lane. The patrol never heard them.

As a result

> A meeting of the Gentlemen to consider the best means to protect the village. Another

> patrol put on – 3 now in number and six men to take turns.

In 1851 a nonconformist school for seventy pupils was opened using Totteridge Park. It catered particularly for the sons of officers or civil servants serving abroad and had very high academic standards.

In 1825 John Wood, who had been Master-in-charge and Domestic Superintendent at Mill Hill School, and John Thorowgood, who had run a preparatory school for Mill Hill, opened a grammar school at the house. They were members of a group of prominent nonconformists who lived in Totteridge at that time including the Puget and Claypon families.

The 1851 census shows John Thorowgood here as a landholder, classical tutor and school master. (He was previously at the school at The Grange above.) By 1881 his widow Sarah was living in Holme Lodge with her son Theodore, a solicitor, who was born in Totteridge in 1845. The Thorowgoods were buried in the dissenters' grave yard at the foot of Totteridge hill.

The Revd Wilkinson, who was principal for many years at the school, lived opposite in Lincoln Lodge, named after the town of his birth. During the last war the house was used by the Women's Land Army who worked on the nearby farms.

Ellern Mede further east is the work of R. Norman Shaw who also designed what until recent years was called New Scotland Yard off Whitehall. He built Ellern Mede in 1877 for William Austin ((1820-1909), a director of a railway company and also of the London Necropolis Company, whose initials are on the front wall. The house was built by William Brass for £4,078 plus Shaw's fee of £220. Some of the mahogany doors are three inches thick and Shaw's concern for high quality was apparent in the stables where the stalls were lined with teak to minimise damage by the horses' hoofs. From 1948 Ellern Mede Farm was let to the A1 Dairies. The house is now a retirement home.

THE TOTTERIDGE MANOR ASSOCIATION

After the death of George Herbert Kemp in 1942, no one was willing to shoulder the responsibilities and expenditure of the lord of the manor and so a group of residents formed the Manor of Totteridge Limited to take over. In 1955, this group combined with the Totteridge Preservation Society to found the Totteridge Manor Association, which acquired the rights to the manorial lands. The Association spends some £45,000 a year on local amenities, mostly litter clearing and land management. It receives no grant from the local authority and is entirely dependent on subscriptions.

Totteridge has six ponds. They are Laurel Farm Pond, Orange Tree Pond, Warren Pond, Long Pond, Ellern Mede Pond and Fairlawn Pond. All are managed by the Totteridge Manor Association.

It is largely because of the vigilance of the Association that Totteridge is such a pleasant place.

TOTTERIDGE GREEN

Thomas E. Collcutt (1840-1924) loved Totteridge. He was one of the most prolific and energetic architects of the late Victorian period itself noted for activity. He designed the Palace Theatre in Cambridge Circus (1888-1891), home for many years now of the musical *Les Miserables*, the Savoy Hotel for D'Oyly Carte (1889), the Wigmore Hall (1901), Lloyd's Registry and part of the Imperial Institute in Kensington (1886). The centenary celebrations for the Wigmore in Spring 2001 provided a reminder of its splendid acoustic properties. Collcutt won the contract to design the P & O Pavilion for the Paris Exhibition of 1900 and designed the interiors of many P & O liners.

He built The Croft on Totteridge Green in 1895 as his own house. It has four reception rooms, six bedrooms, six bathrooms, two guest cloakrooms, a swimming pool, a 2-bedroom cottage annexe and a flat. Collcutt obviously used the house as an advertisement for his work. Also at Totteridge Green he designed Strathearn (1899) for A.B. Smith – now Consolata College.

He also designed Fairspeir, a house which is something of a mystery. The designs for "a house at Totteridge for Miss Jones" are dated 13 July 1899, the date that appears on the decorative plaque bearing her initials. However, no evidence exists to identify her and the relevant rate books are lost. The small size of the house and reticent design have obscured its architectural importance. The authoritative *Das Englische Haus* says "There is no display or sign of high living, no outward showmanship or magnificence, no luxury or opulence." Reversing the mid- Victorian fashion for spires, battlements and elaborate

183. Lynch House on Totteridge Green (see p.136).

ceilings, Collcutt planned houses that are comfortable to live in, easy to work and pleasant to look at. The Lloyd sisters lived in the house from 1933 until the 1990s.

In 1911 Collcutt was asked by his friend Major Boulton to design a house for him. This was Woodcroft, just to the west of The Croft, which has since been demolished and replaced by Grovelands. For Totteridge Park he designed the stable block, which has since been converted into a house called The Paddocks. He designed the Lynch House (*ill. 183*) in 1904 for Anthony Howard whom he had met in his work for P & O. Howard called it the Lynch House after the house where he had spent his childhood.

Both Collcutt and his wife are buried at Totteridge.

The Old House on the corner of the Green dated from the early seventeenth century – the original basement still exists. In 1850 John Mackay leased it and used the two-acre garden as a commercial nursery. By that time Georgian architecture was out of fashion and it would have been quite in order for a gardener to use such a property. He was in charge of Queen Victoria's gardens.

His son, also John Mackay, had East Ridge, running along Totteridge Lane, built in his father's back garden.

About 1910 the buildings to the south side were used by the Patent Steam Laundry and Carpet Beating Company which used the Green to lay out carpets to dry.

The double rows of trees on the Green were set out to improve the view from Poynter's Grove.

The nearby Green Lodge, known locally as the Ginger Bread House, is one of four gatehouses to Copped Hall. It was substantially refaced about 1885.

Laurel Farm at the southern end of Totteridge Green was destroyed by a bomb on 4 August 1944. The house was rebuilt as Home Farm and a neighbouring house was renamed Laurel Farm House. The fields for Laurel Farm ran as far as the Dollis Brook.

The first Orange Tree was opened by John Bemon in 1665. In 1756 it, and the Three Horseshoes are described as having "2 beds and 2 stables, Horseshoes, 1 bed and 2 stables." Totteridge's second pub, The Crown, is shown with 2 beds and 1 stable. Its exact location is not certain.

The Three Horse Shoes Inn is a reference to the

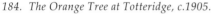

184. The Orange Tree at Totteridge, c.1905.

smithy that stood for years behind the school. In the 1840s the smith was Thomas Briers and his wife ran a small school which legend says was in the smithy.

A Charles Baldwin and his family lived in one room of a cottage on the Green. When he died in 1853 an inventory was made of his property. This is a list of his possessions:

2 mattresses, 3 sheets, 1 iron pot, 1 plate, 2 spoons, 2 trestles, 2 boards, 2 cups, 1 knife, 1 fork. They had no chair. They would probably have eaten straight from the pot. After his death the family were taken into Barnet workhouse.

POYNTERS GROVE

Poynters Grove stood opposite the Green. It was owned by the Puget family for nearly 100 years. John David Puget (1760 to 1805) married Catherine Hawkins and entered the family firm of Puget and Bainbridge, bankers, in 1777. In 1790 aged only 30 he became a Governor of the Bank of England.

He lived in John Street, Holborn and in 1799 bought Poynters Grove as his country house. It was described as "a mansion house with coach houses, stables, barns and other out houses, 2 closes of meadow containing by estimation 12 acres, also Wood Grove of 8 acres and Churchfield of 8½ acres".

The house had been built for Lady Gurney in 1652. While in the possession of a later owner, Mrs Williams, the grounds had been laid out by Capability Brown and included two fish ponds. At the same time a double avenue of trees was planted along Totteridge Green in order to enhance the view. A subsequent owner Catherine Puget, widow of John Puget, born about 1765, was a member of one of Ireland's leading families. She had a beautiful singing voice and was a celebrated beauty. She had met King William IV who was so struck by her that twenty years later he still talked of her. Her portrait by Gainsborough hung for many years in the house.

After her husband John Puget had died of a stroke while getting on his horse, she sold their Holborn house and spent the rest of her life in Totteridge. In 1819 she paid for a small brick chapel in the village, intended for her estate labourers. This is now Chapel Cottage. In 1827 she provided more money for a second and larger dissenters' chapel at the foot of the hill.

She was particularly known for her good works. On the day of her death, 11 February 1842, she failed to come down for the evening meal and she was discovered lying on the floor of her bedroom clutching one of the little packets of coins that she always carried to help the needy.

Her son was John Hey Puget (1803-1867) who married his cousin Isabella Hawkins in August 1826 settling £40,000 on her. They lived in a large house at 31 Sussex Square, Brighton. He was a close friend of Joseph Sortain, a Weslyan preacher and together they founded a school in Ship Street, Brighton in 1840. As well as paying the teacher's salary, he gave each child a set of clothes at Christmas.

After the death of his mother, he moved to Poynters Grove where he continued the family tradition of helpfulness. It was said that he made up the wages of any working man who was injured or too ill to work normally and he employed rural missionaries in Totteridge and Whetstone.

Puget bought up more land and eventually owned about 152 acres extending from the church to Dollis Brook and from Totteridge Lane to Mays Lane and Barnet Lane.

He died in April 1867 aged 64 and his widow died in 1882 aged 85.

His son, John, who was born in 1827, bought a commission in the army, served in India from 1849 and was a lieutenant at the siege of Sebastopol in the Crimean War. Returning to India he served as a captain during the Indian Mutiny. He was made FRGS in 1862 for his services to exploration and map-making in India. In 1882 Colonel Puget moved into Poynters Grove and built yet another church in Oakleigh Road. He died in 1894 and is buried at the Islington cemetery in Finchley.

Poynters Grove then went to his nephew who sold it to Mrs Geraldine Harmsworth, a member of the newspaper family. The house was pulled down in 1936 when the clock was given to the parish church. Harmsworth Way, Northcliffe Drive, Pine Grove and The Paddocks are all built on the estate. Geraldine Cottage on the corner of Harmsworth Way is entirely appropriate.

THE DISSENTERS' CHAPEL

The old dissenters' chapel (*see above*) consisted of "a large preaching room with two small chambers at the end", with a crypt beneath. A burial ground was opened in 1831 and was last used in 1885. The first minister was Thomas Pinkerton who lived in the Manse at the rear. At that time worshippers from Whetstone had to wade Dollis Brook because Finchley and Totteridge could not

185. *The Dissenters' Chapel in Totteridge Lane. It was opened in 1828 with money provided by Catherine Puget.*

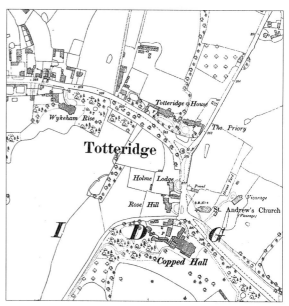

186. *The centre of Totteridge in 1895.*

agree about sharing the cost of building a footbridge. A man used to carry people across the brook in a wheelbarrow for one farthing a time. John Puget paid for a wooden footbridge to be erected in 1843.

There is a striking example of the ferocity of religious differences in the 1860s in the chapel minutes. "This evil man has left us and joined the Baptists. Has dangerous ideas. Means must be found to destroy him."

After the opening of the congregational church in Oakleigh Park the chapel became redundant. It was eventually leased by George Sherwood in 1919 who at first sold surplus army lorries and graduated then to become an Austin agent with show rooms in Finchley. The chapel building became derelict until 1939 when it was bought by Barnet Council as an ARP post.

After the war it was disused until 2001 when Elder Court was built on the site.

To the rear of the chapel was a day school and master's house. For 45 years the teacher was Thomas Reynolds, a remarkable man, now completely forgotten. He was born in Spitalfields in 1818, apprenticed as a printer and educated himself at a mechanics' institute, doing well enough to train as a teacher at Borough Road College. In those days the course lasted three months. "Our aim", wrote the principal, "is to keep them occupied incessantly from five in the morning till nine or ten at night". "Not surpris-

ingly", he commented plaintively, "this sometimes has an adverse effect on their health". After Reynolds left college he came to the attention of J.H. Puget at his Brighton school (see above) and when Puget came to Totteridge, Reynolds came with him.

He had an unusual way of keeping discipline. He did not use corporal punishment. Instead he had a system of punishments and rewards. Talkers, players and idlers had to wear a paper hat appropriately marked. Dirty boys were brought to the front and publicly washed. However, good work and behaviour was rewarded by a system of merit tickets which could be exchanged at the end of each term for clothes or books. Puget, of course, provided the money.

Reynolds was an exceptionally kind man with a gift for clear explanation. Many former pupils kept in touch with him throughout their lives, particularly after the school leaving age was raised to 12. Like all school masters he was poorly paid. and he also worked as a part time reporter for the *Barnet Press* and ran a small stationer's business about where Barclay's Bank now stands.

SOUTH HERTS GOLF CLUB

South Herts Golf Club was formed about 1899 out of the Muswell Hill Golf Club whose original course was about a mile from Colney Hatch and was threatened by housing development. Another disadvantage was that their course was on land owned by the church and members were not allowed to use it on Sundays.

Land was therefore leased at Totteridge in 1899, resulting in a cost of about £4,000 for the land, the course and the building. Fees for the original members were three guineas and for new arrivals, five guineas and when membership reached 250 in 1900 the fee was increased to seven guineas. An interesting point concerning the religious outlook of the day was the club rule that "no caddie or other servant shall be employed on Sundays".

It was not until 1928 that the club was able to buy the freehold of the land at a cost of £21,000. Mr Griffiths of the Green Man agreed to provide on-site catering of a two-shilling cold lunch and a sixpenny tea on Saturdays. Once again religion had the last word and no refreshments were allowed on Sundays.

Today the club covers 120 acres and several club buildings have been put up over the years, most notably the replacements for those damaged by bombing in the last war and a disastrous fire in 1959. The main course has undergone changes and a short 9-hole course, which had been introduced in 1934 was improved in 1969.

By 2001 the club had around 800 members, men and women from many parts of the world. About 15 permanent staff look after administration, catering and ground maintenance.

The club has had the benefit of two world class professionals.

Harry William Vardon was born in Jersey on 9 May 1870. He was the fourth of eight children and left school at thirteen to become a gardener. He started to play golf at the age of seven with home made clubs and large white marbles but he developed his legendary skills by watching others rather than by having lessons. The overlap grip on the shaft which he developed is known throughout the world as the 'Vardon grip'. He was appointed professional at Bury Golf Club in Lancashire in 1891 and won the British Open Golf Championship a record six times – in 1896, 1898, 1899, 1903, 1911 and 1914 – and also won the US Open in 1900.

187. Harry Vardon driving off at the North Middlesex Golf Club, though he was a professional at the South Herts Club in Totteridge.

Harry moved to Totteridge in 1902 and was to remain there for the rest of his life. He was buried at St Andrew's Totteridge in 1937 and a blue plaque was later put up on his house in Totteridge Lane.

David James Rees (1913-1983), known by everyone except his family as Dai, was born at Fontgary, Glamorganshire. His father was a professional golfer and young David played his first game at the age of five – his talent was such that he became a professional at 15. He achieved considerable success in the 1930s but his career was interrupted by the war. In 1946, he was offered the position of professional at South Herts. In the summer of 1955, Dai achieved one of golf's greatest honours when he was appointed captain of Britain's Ryder Cup team. Although they lost that time the British team won the cup in 1957, a feat not to be repeated until 1985. The recognition that followed that year included the CBE and the winning of the BBC's Sports Personality of the Year award.

On his death, his ashes were scattered in the Garden of Rest at Totteridge Church.

TAILPIECE

From the Totteridge parish records 1780:

> Here is a pretty job, the wooden leg overseer at Whetstone brought John Bunyan and left him at my door a very cold night knowing the folks at Totteridge are very good natured.

Appendix
Population figures

FINCHLEY

1769	900 (est.)		
1801	1,503	1901	22,126
1811	1,292	1911	39,419
1821	2,349	1921	46,716
1831	3,210	1931	59,113
1841	3,664	1941	not available
1851	4,120	1951	69,991
1861	4,937	1961	69,370
1871	7,146 *	1971	15,643
1881	11,191	1981	13,775
1891	16, 647	1991	13,983

Notes
* Figure includes about 1,000 migrant workers on the railway.
  Boundary changes in 1971

FRIERN BARNET

1801	432	1901	11,566
1811	487	1911	14,924
1821	534	1921	17,375
1831	615	1931	23,101
1841	849	1941	not available
1851	974	1951	29,163
1861	3,344 *	1961	28,813
1871	4,347	1971	15,108
1881	6,424	1981	14,474
1891	9,173	1991	14,564

Notes
* Increase partly caused by opening of Colney Hatch Asylum.
  Boundary changes in 1971

TOTTERIDGE

1801	280	1901	844
1811	368		
1821	490		
1831	595	1931	1,024
1841	409	1941	not available
1851	595 *	1951	4,500
1861	575	1961	5,839
1871	474	1971	15,641
1881	657	1981	15,290
1891	795	1891	15,325

Notes
* Note drop in population in 1841 and 1871 caused by cholera epidemics.
  Boundary changes in 1971.

Whetstone

1841	440
1951	8,724
1961	8,485

INDEX
Asterisks denote illustrations or captions

ABBOTTS GARDENS 54
Acres, Birt 87
Advance Cleaners 43
Aethelred, King 8
Aggangeat 8
Albert, Prince 84
Albert Place 32
Albert Street School 99-100
Albert Terrace 31-32
Albion Estates Co. 87
Albion Road 87
Alcokes Lane 18
Alder, J.S. 99
Alder School 21, *52
Ale Taster 22
Alexandra Grove 32, 92
Alexandra Ladies' College 32
All Saints church, Myddelton Park 123
All Saints girls' School 123, *126
Allandale Avenue 24
Allen, Edward 60
Allen, Sir Thomas 60-61
Almshouses 41, 50, *50, 78
Angels Farm 30
Arcadia Avenue 36
Arcadia Skating Rink *35, 36
Archaeological finds 7-8
Archery 114
Arden, Edward 61
Arden Road 24, 61
Argyle Road *90
Arlington Cottages 102
Arrowsmith family 134
Arsenal football club 74
Ashurst Road 74
Athenaeum, The 124
Athenaeum Cinema 41
Athenaeum Road 124
Attfield family 122-123, *122
Austin, William 134
Avenue House 26, 27, *27, 28
Avenue, The 26, *27, 86
Avern Street 10, 75
Avondale Avenue 97
Aylmer Road 9, 63

BACON family 74, 78, 110
Baines, George & Co. 86
Bald Faced Stag 37
Baldwin, Charles 137
Ballard, Henry 30
Ballards Lane 11, 14, *15, *18, 23, 27, 30-32, 33, 54, 63, 88, 92
Baptists 92
Barclays bank, Whetstone 117, *118
Barfield Avenue 124
Barham, Sir George 24, 26
Barnet 8
Barnet By-pass 63
Barnet Health Authority 69
Barnet Hill 11
Barnet Press *22, 123, 127, 128, 138

Barnett & Birch 46, 55
Baronsmere 43
Barratt, Sir Albert 129
Barratt, S.G. 129-130
Basing, Adam de 60, 104, 113
Basings Ponds 104
Bass, William 115
Batho, William 88
Baume, Pierre 78
Baxendale (road) 114
Baxendale, Joseph 12, 80, 113-114, *113, *114
Beaconsfield Road 72, 86
Beard, Mary 85
Bedford, Ian 99
Bedford Road 44
Beis Yaakov Primary Schools 21
Bell, Charles 32
Bemon, John 136
Bensley, Thomas 74
Berger, Miss 117, 119
Berman, M. & Co. 117
Bernays, Revd Stewart 62
Bethune Park 78
Bettstyle 8, 71, 82
Bianna, High Road 100
Bibbesworth Manor 23
Bibbesworth Road 24
Billing, A. 18
Bishop Douglass Secondary School 54, 67
Bishop's Avenue 9, 40, *40
Bishop's Gate 18
Bishop's Park 9
Black Bull, High Road 127
Blackett's Brook 78
Blomfield, Charles 114
Boulton, Miss T. *88
Boulton, Sir Samuel 131
Bow Lane 65
Bowes Road 8
Bramber Road 74
Brass, William 134
Brent Lodge 88
Brewerton, Charles 128
Briarfield Avenue 56
Bridgemour, Richard 109
Briers, Thomas 137
Britannia Road 114
British Empire Films 110-111
British Famous films 110-111
Brockley Hill 7, 8
Brook Farm 117
Brooklands School 21, 51
Brown Boveri 87
Brown, John & Henson 72
Brown, Lancelot 'Capability' 137
Brown, Richard 109
Brownlow Road 33
Brownswell 51
Brunswick Park Road 8
Brydges, James, Duke of Chandos 125
Buckingham Avenue 127
Bull and Butcher 120, 121, *121
Bull Inn, Whetstone 11
Burridge, Mrs 90
Burtonwood Engineering 104
Buses *13, 14, *14
Butlin, E. Barlow 99
Buxted Road 74

CAMBRIDGE CLOSE 87
Cambridge Instrument Co. 87
Campe, Lawrence 78
Campe almshouses 78, *81
Carey, Sir William 71, 72
Carlisle Place 86
Carnegie Trust 73
Caroe, W.D. 28, 87
Carrimore Six-Wheelers 104
Castle, Revd E. 93
Castle, William 12
Causeway, The 41
Cavendish Avenue 28
Cedar Court 88, *90
Chambers, William 120
Chandos Avenue 125, *126
Chandos, Duke of *see* James Brydges
Chapel Cottage 137
Chapel Street 51
Chaplin & Horne 12
Charcoal burning 130
Charles II, King 72
Cherry Tree Woods 9
Chessington Avenue 24
Chislehurst Avenue 67
Choppin, Francis 12
Christ Church school, Stanhope Road 96-97
Christ Church United Reform church 86
Christ Church, Finchley Common 88
Christ Church, High Road 91, *91
Christ's College *19, 20-21, *20-21, 23, 30
Christchurch Avenue 92
Church End 18-36
Church Hill, East Barnet 7
Church Lane 55
Church Path 110
Churchfield estate 91
Cinemas 33, *33, *34, 40-41, 91, 93, 103
Civil Defence 27
Claigmar Gardens 58
Claigmar Vineyard 58
Claremont Park 24
Clark's Bakeries 43
Clarke, J. 123
Clarke, Sir Simon Haughton 123
Claverly, Ballards Lane 32
Claverly Grove 32
Claybrook Close 51
Clements' Nursery 19, 21, 24
Cliffe, Edward 131
Clulow family 67
Coaches 11, 12, *12, 93
Coathouse Farm 97
Cobley family 67
Cobley's Farm 67
Coldfall Wood 9, 48
Coldharbour 12, 110
Coliseum cinema 40, *41
Collcutt, Thomas E. 135-136
College Farm 24, *24
Collier, W.G. 86
Collins, Margaret 98
Collins, Thomas 9
Collins, Thomas 98

Collins, W. 43
Colney Hatch 10, 71
Colney Hatch Asylum 16, 82, *83, 84-85, *84
Colney Hatch Gas Co. 123, *124
Colney Hatch Lane 71, 82, *83
Commons (*see also* Finchley Common) 9
Compton, Denis 70
Compton School 70, 100
Congregational churches 45, 53
Conservative Land Society 32
Consolata College 135
Cooper, Edward Philip 61
Cooper, Jonathan 127
Co-operative store, High Road 100
Co-partnership Tenants 63
Copewood, Thomas 123
Copped Hall 131, *131, *132, 136
Coppetts Farm 87
Coppies Grove 86
Copps Dairy *116, 117
Cornwall Avenue 32
Cornwall House, Ballards Lane
Costa, Joseph da *132
Cottager's Chapel 92
Cottam, Lawrence 98
Council housing 59, 69, 124
Court House, Nether Street 90
Courthouse Farm Dairy 90
Cowley, R.E. 133
Creighton Avenue 44
Crescent Road 75
Croft, The, Totteridge Green 135
Cromwell Road 87
Crossway 69
Crown, The, High Road 106
Cuckold's Haven 49
Curtis, Sir William and Mary 84
Cyprus Road 24

DABBS, William 40
Dale Grove 92
Dale Grove school 92
Darlands, Totteridge 131
Daukes, S.W. 84
Davies, William 119
Dawber, Sir E. Guy 131
Day, Charles 29
De Dion 104
Deansway 54
Deard's 56, *57, 58, 70
Denison Close 55
Derwent House 110
Dickens, Charles 67
Dickens Avenue 67
Direct Dry Cleaners 124
Dissenters' chapel, Totteridge 137-138, *138
Dixon, Thomas 109
Doggett, John 122, 123
Dollis Avenue 28
Dollis Brook 9, 24, 28, *28, *29, 62, 88, 129, 137
Dollis Park 28
Domesday Survey 9
Donovan, John 80
Duck, Walter 18
Ducksetters Lane 18, 63

Dunger, Henry 70
Dunger Place 59, 70

EAST BARNET Gas Co. 123, *124, 127
East End British School 51
East End Road 53-59
East Finchley 37-52
East Finchley Baptist Church 44
East Finchley Board School 51, *52
East Finchley Library 45, *46
East Finchley Methodist Church 44
East Finchley Picturedrome 40
East Finchley station *16, 37, *38, 43
East Ridge, Totteridge Lane 136
East Weald, Bishop's Avenue 40
Edgware, Highgate & London Railway 16
Electricity Works, Squires Lane 58-59, *59
Elizabeth I, Queen 71
Ellern Mede, Totteridge 134
Elm Grange, Nether Street (1) 88
Elm Grange, Nether Street (2) 88
Elm Park Road 30, 88
Elm Villa 88
Elmshurst, East End Road *54, 55
Elmshurst Crescent 55
Emberson, Septimus 72
EMC Advertising 12
Enclosure Act 1816 9
Essex House 33
Essex Park 33
Esting, Simon 104
Etchingham Lodge 33
Etchingham Park 33
Eversleigh Road 88
Express Dairy 24, *25, 26

FAIRHOLME Gardens 24
Fairlawn Avenue 40
Fairspeir, Totteridge Green 135
Falkland House, Ballards Lane 32, 88
Falloden Way 63
Fallow Corner 42, 67
Fallow Court, Nether Street 30
Fallow Court Avenue 67
Fallow Farm 33, 67
Fallow Lodge 67
Farnham Close 128
Ferncroft Avenue 82
Ferret and Trouser Leg 30
Ferrours Lane 51
Ffoxe family 106
Fields, Gracie 40
Film making 110-111
Finchley: geology 7, *7; prehistory 7-8
Finchley Borough 23
Finchley Carnival 36, *36, *57, 69
Finchley Catholic Grammar School 104
Finchley Catholic High School

104
Finchley Central Station 16, *17
Finchley Charities 22, 23, 29, 30, 31, 41, 50, 53, 61
Finchley Choral Society 99
Finchley Church End Station 16, *17
Finchley Common 7, 9, 51, 64, 69, 88, 106
Finchley Common Congregational Church 92
Finchley Conservative Association 33
Finchley Co-partnership Society 24
Finchley County School *66, 67
Finchley Court 33
Finchley Drill Hall 64
Finchley Football Club 65
Finchley Hall 18, 20, 23
Finchley Leisure Centre *66
Finchley Local Board 30
Finchley Lodge 97
Finchley Manor House 60-61, *60
Finchley Meeting Hall 32, 33
Finchley Memorial Hospital 68-69, *69, 88, 103
Finchley Park (road) 103
Finchley Park 23, 103
Finchley Presbyterian Lawn Tennis Club 54
Finchley Press 41, 96, 104
Finchley Society 28
Finchley Spa 63
Finchley Urban District Council 23, 30, 59
Finchley Village *23, 24
Finchley Way 88
Finchley Wood 9
Finchley Youth Theatre 45
Fiott, John 134
Fir Cottage, Ballards Lane 23, 54
Fire fighting and stations 21, *22, 32, 43, 51, 72-73, 117, *118
First World War 27, 33, 85, 96, 104
Fitzalan Road 24
Five Bells, East End 42, 53, *53
Flach, Harry 96
Fletcher, Cyril 72
Folly Brook 129
Fortis Green estate 43
Fountains Court 33
Franklin Close 127
Frederick's Place 102
Freehold Community Centre 87, *87
Freehold Estate 87
Frenchman's Farm 78
Friary Park 71, 72, 74, 75, 78
Friern Barnet 8, 9, 10, 71-80
Friern Barnet almshouses 78
Friern Barnet & District Local History Society 80

Friern Barnet County School 75
Friern Barnet District Board 72, 75, 78
Friern Barnet Hospital *see*

Colney Hatch Asylum
Friern Barnet infants' school 80
Friern Barnet Lane 82
Friern Barnet Road 71, 72
Friern Barnet Town Hall 72, *72, *73
Friern House, Friern Barnet Lane *76, 117
Friern Lodge 78
Friern Manor Farm *76
Friern Mount Drive 127
Friern Watch, High Road 68, 102-103
Friern Watch Avenue 103
Frith Manor 90
Frost, James 51
Fulham 9
Furniture Land 103
Fursby Avenue 88
Fursby House 88

GAINSBOROUGH Court 90
Gamage, Albert 61
Gannick Corner 11
Garden Hill, Totteridge 133
Gatehouse, Highgate 10
Gateway House 36
Gaumont Cinema 92, 93, *95, *96
Gelder, Bill 86
George Crescent 87
George, The, East Finchley 43, *43
George, The, Totteridge Lane 43, 120
Gerrard, Henry 97
Gibbet 48
Gilmour, Robert 109
Glebe Lands 64
Glenthorne, Bishop's Avenue 40
Glenthorne Road 75, 86
Gomvill, Sir William 75
Goodyear, Ald. Frederick and family 23, 30, 67, 92
Gordon Road 30
Goslings 103
Grand Hall Cinema 93, *94
Grange Avenue 134
Grange, The, Nether Street 92
Grange, The, Totteridge Lane 133, 134
Grange, The, Whetstone 50, 97, 127
Granville Road 30, 33, 67, *68
Grass Farm 9, 28
Gravel Hill 23, 30
Gray Brothers *39
Great North Road 8, 10, *10, 11, 18, 37, 67
Great Northern Cemetery 16, 85
Great Northern Motors 100
Great Northern Railway 16, 37, *38, 82, 120
Green Lodge, Totteridge 136
Green Man, East Finchley 51
Green Man, Whetstone *107, 123, *123, 139
Green Way 90
Griffin inn *108, 109
Griffith, Diana 129

Grimaldi, Joseph 67, *67
Grocott, S. 128
Grosvenor Road 88
Grove, The 32
Grove House, Ballards Lane 27, 32
Groves, Sir Charles 124
Gruneisen Road 33
Gurney, Lady 137
Gwyn, Nell 72
Gynne, Rhoda 92

HABERSHON Brothers 78
Hadley 7
Halliwick 71, 82, *82
Halliwick manor house 69, 82
Halliwick Road 87
Hamilton Francis A. 24, 88
Hamilton, Henry 32
Hamilton, Mrs 32, 33
Hamilton Court 91
Hamilton Way 88
Hampden Road 87
Hampstead Garden Suburb 55
Hand and Flower 117, *118
Harmsworth, Mrs Geraldine 137
Harmsworth Way 137
Harper's bakery 120, *121
Hartland Road 73
Harvey, Len 127
Haslemere Gardens 24
Hawkins, Rev. Henry 85
Hawkins, Isabella 137
Hawkins, Joseph 117, *118
Hay production 37
Haybourne, John 122
Hazlehurst, Edmund 32
Head, Marion 80
Headborough 22
Heal family 28-29
Hemington Avenue 75
Hemmings Lands 125
Hendon & District Arch. Soc. 7, 8, 60
Hendon Avenue 24
Hendon Lane 18, *19, 21, 23, 29
Hendon Lane Farm 24
Hertford Lodge 28, 44
Hewart, Lord 133
High Road 7, 12, 21, *38, *39, 44, 93, *93, *104, *105, *106, 107, *108, *109, *111, 112.
Highgate 9
Highwaymen 48
Hill family 82
Hill Crescent 90
Hillside Avenue
Hillside Farm 74
Hilsdon, Henry 32
Hilton Avenue 96
Hog Market 43, *43, *44, 54
Hog Road 45
Hogman's Hern 98
Holden, Henry 101
Holden Road 91, 99
Holdenhurst 67
Holdenhurst Avenue 67
Holdenhurst Road 33
Hollickwood 9
Hollickwood Avenue 82
Hollickwood Park 87
Hollickwood school 87

Holly Cottage, College Road 21
Holly Park Estate 86, *86
Holly Park School 75, 86, *86
Hollyfield Avenue 82
Hollyfield estate 74
Holman, Ebenezer 68, 102
Holme Lodge, Totteridge 133, 134
Holmesdale Road 86
Holy Trinity School 43, 45, 55
Homefield cottages 54
Howard Bros. 117
Howard, Anthony 136
Hudgell, E. 93
Hutton Grove 92

INCOGNITO Theatre 86
Ingleway *70
Ingram Road 43
Isolation Hospital 70
Ivy House, High Road 109

JAMES, Alex 74
Jason, David 86
Jelks, William 82, 97, 127
Jersey Farm 90
Johnston, Maria 78
Joiner's Arms 23
Jolly Blacksmith 37

KEMP, George Herbert 131, 135
Kendrick, Hohn 12
King Edward Hall 23
Kinge, Elizabeth 26
Kingsford, Ellen 67
Kingsway 14, 93, *94
Kinloss Gardens 24
Kirk, Sir John 67
Kitchener Road 44
Kitson, Fanny 93
Knights Hospitaller 9, 71
Knights Templar 27

LA DELIVRANCE 62, *63
Ladds, John 33
Lambert, William 98
Lambert Road 44
Langhorne, John 33
Langton Avenue 127
Lansdown Road 88
Laurel Drive 90
Laurel Farm 90, 136
Lauzan family 128
Leader, William 90
Lendon, Revd. Abel 131
Leo Baeck College 61
Libraries 27, *27, 45, 73, *73, *74, 101, *101
Limes, The, High Road 109
Link Road 86
Lloyd, Robert 110
Lloyd George, David 62
Lodge Lane 97
London General Omnibus Co. 12
London Land Co. 73
Long Lane 51, *52
Longland Drive 90
Loring Road 75
Lyle, William 40
Lynch House, Totteridge Green *135, 136

Lyndhurst Avenue 82
Lyndhurst Gardens 28
Lyndhurst Road 24
Lynn's Rents 117, *118, *120
Lyttelton Road 63

MACKAY, John 136
Mail coaches 10, *10
Mainland, George 105
Manning, Cardinal Henry 131, 133
Manning, William 131
Manor Cottage Tavern 56, *57
Manor Farm, Finchley 56, 58
Manor Farm, Friern Barnet 74, 75, *77, *78
Manor Farm Dairy *19
Manorhill School 67, 70
Manors 9
Manorside School 59
Market Parade 93
Market Place 43, *44
Marsham family 133
Marshman, Mrs 92
Martin Primary School 45, *45
Martyn family 113
Mayfield Avenue *103
McCurd lorry factory 104
Mellor, B. 115
Merry Millers 43
Methodist churches 32, 44, 88
Metropolitan Electric Tramways 14
Middlesex County Council 21, 30, 67, 73
Middlesex County Pauper Lunatic Asylum *see* Colney Hatch Asylum
Middlesex Cricket Club Indoor School 58
Miles, Rev. Henry 67, *125
Miles, John 75, *77, 80, 123
Miles Way 124
Miller, Agnes 104
Milligan, Spike 28
Mills Shopfitting 110, *113
Montrose Road 33
Morecambe, Eric 101, *101
Morley's Farm 124
Mortimer, Lily *26
Mortuaries 70, 78
Mosely Dene, Woodside Park Road 101
Moss Hall 92
Moss Hall estate 30, 92
Moss Hall Grove 92
Moss Hall school 92
Moss Hall Terrace 92
Mosse, John 92
Moulton, Thomas 127
Mountain, Peter and Ann 12, 93, 109
Mountfield Road 28, 63
Muswell Hill Farm 87
Muswell Hill Golf Club 139
Mutton Brook 9
Myddelton Park 75, 123
National Hospital for the Paralysed and the Insane 40

NATIONAL Land Corporation 75

National Provincial Bank 93
Neale Close 55
Needham, Thomas 99
Nelson, P. 93
Nether Street 24, 30, 88, *88, 90, 92
New Bohemia 33, 35
New River Company 75
Newcombe Estate Co. 103
Newgate Lane 18
Newman, Francis 120
Newman, H. 12
Newman, T.C. 92
Newman, Thomas 120
Newton cycle shop, St John's Row *110
Nicholson, Archibald 134
Nicholson Sir Charles 18, 131, 133
Nicholson, Sir Sydney 133-134
North Circular Road 51, 56, 62, *62
North London Hospice 104
North Middlesex Golf Club 74, *76, 78, *80
North Mount 110
North Road elementary school 45
Northcliffe Drive 137
Northern Line 37
Northiam estate 90
Northside School 86, 100
Northumberland Road 8
Norton, J. 91

OAK LANE Health Centre 49
Oakfield Road 58
Oakleigh Infants' School 124
Oakleigh Park Estate 123
Oakleigh Park North 123
Oakleigh Park South 123
Oakleigh Park station 16
Oakleigh Road North 124
Oakleigh Road South 8
Odell, Thomas 43
Odeon Cinema, High Road 103
Old Bohemia 33, *34, *35
Old House, Totteridge Green 136
Old King of Prussia *31
Oldham Estates 82
Orange Tree, Friern Barnet 71, *71, 72
Orange Tree, Totteridge 136, *136
Orchard Lodge 92
Our Lady of Lourdes Catholic School 67
Overseer of the Poor 22
Oxford Gardens 124

PADDOCKS, The 137
Pardes House 21
Parish government 22
Park Farm 55
Park Farm Close 55
Park Hall 43
Park Road Hotel 12, 93, *93
Parker, Robert 109
Parvin, Frank 134
Patent Steam Laundry 136
Paul, Robert 87
Peacock family 90

Pearson, John L. 73
Pegrum, H.B. 21
Pentstemon Close 88
Percy Road 91
Pert, William 103
Pert Close 87
Petworth Road 74
Pfotzer, Helen 128
Philip, Prince *61
Philipson, J.T. 21
Phillipson House 92
Pickford's 12, 113-114
Pike, Ald. 45
Pilgrim Property Co. 106
Pine Grove 137
Pinkerton, Thomas 137
Pitcher, J.D. 40
Pizza Express 109
Place Lane 58
Plowman & Co 54
Plunknett, George 61
Pointalls 41, 50
Policing and police stations 32, 102, *116, 117, 102, 134
Pollard Road 75
Poor, treatment of 41-42, 54, 60
Poor houses 54
Poor Sisters of Nazareth 54
Pope, George 32
Pope's Alley 32
Pope's garage 32
Popham, Sir John 71
Pound House, Totteridge 130
Pound Road 43
Poynters Grove, Totteridge 136, 137
Pratt, John 128
Pratt, Robert 30
Prime, Jack 111
Prior, Robert 97, *100
Priory, The, Friern Barnet Lane *72, 73
Priory, The, Totteridge 130, *130
Prize fighting 53
Prospect Place 43
Puget family 92, 137, 138
Pymmes Brook 78, 85

QUEEN'S HEAD, Church End 11, 20, 22-23, 26
Queens Avenue 124
Queenswell School 80, 124

RADIO RENTALS 93
Railway Hotel 30, *31, 65
Railways 16, *16-17
Raleigh Drive 75
Raleigh, Sir Walter 71, 75
Ramsden Road 73
Rasper Road 117
Ravensdale Avenue 101, 103
Red Lion estate 49
Red Lion Hill 49
Rees, Dai 139
Regent's Canal Company 9
Regent's Park Road 11, *14, 26, 28, 63
Rex cinema 40, *41
Reynolds, Thomas 138
Richardson, E.W. 75
Road maintenance 10, 11
Roads 10-12

Roberts, Edward 29
Roman period 8
Rose Hill, Totteridge 133
Rose's oil shop *111
Rosemary Avenue 56
Rosemont Avenue 14
Rothermere, Lord 62
Rough Lots 64, *64
Ruffins Bridge 78

SAILOR'S Refreshment rooms *127
Sainsbury, George 40
Sainsbury's 100
St Albans abbey 8
St Albans' preparatory school 104
St Andrew's church, Totteridge *129, 130, 139
St Barnabas church 99
St James's church, Friern Barnet 71, 74, 75, 78, *79, 106, 120
St James's school 75, 78, 80, *81
St John's Avenue 82
St John's church, Friern Barnet 73
St John's church, Whetsone 114, *115
St John's school, Crescent Road 75
St John's school, Totteridge Lane 114-115, *115
St Luke's church, Mountfield Road 28
St Mary's church, Finchley 9, 18, *19, 54, 61
St Mary's RC church 45, *45
St Mary's schools 29, *30
St Marylebone & Finchley Turnpike Trust 11
St Marylebone Cemetery 55-56, *55, *56
St Michael's Catholic Grammar School 92
St Pancras and Islington cemeteries 46, *47
St Pancras Court 46, *47
St Paul's church, Long Lane 33, 88
St Paul's Road 86
St Peter's church 87
St Peter's school 87
Salisbury Arms, Barnet 12
Salisbury Avenue 24
Salmon, John 111
Salvation Army 44
Salvin, Anthony 20, 45, 54, *54, 55
Sandwell Ladies' College 90
Sanger, 'Lord' George 55, 56
Sanny, John 109
Sanny, Thomas 53, 103
Sarnes Barnet 82
Saunders, James 120
Saxon period 8
Schools 29, 45, 51, 54, 59, 67, 69, 70, 75, 78, 80, 82, 87, 90, 92, 96, 99-100, 104, 114-115, 124, 133, 134
Searle, Messrs 92
Second World War 27, 43, 56, 68-69, 85, 99, 117, 134, 136, 138

Sellars Hall 88
Sellers, Peter 41
Sewage and rubbish disposal 70, 78, 85
Seymour Road 33
Shaw, R. Norman 134
Sheephouse Farm 9, 24, *24
Shenton, Frederick 110
Sherwood Street 75
Sherwood, George 100, 138
Shree Aden Depala Mitra-mandel group 45
Simmons, Sydney 75
Simmons Way 124
Simms Gardens *50
Simms Motors 49-50, *49
Sisters of the Good Shepherd 54
Sisters of the Poor Child Jesus 92
Sisters of the Society of Marie Auxiliatrice 61
Skating rink 103, *103, *104
Skiva Primary School 61, *61
Slums 87
Smith, A.B. 135
Smith, Edward 104
Smith, George 82
Smith, George Knights 73, 74, 86
Smith, Henry 82
South Herts Golf Club 139, *139
South Mount 110
Southernhay, Totteridge 133
Southgate and Colney Hatch station 16
Southgate Park 73
Southover estate 90
Spotted Dog 110
Spring Close 90
Squires Lane 58-59, *58
Squires Lane school 59
Stage Coaches 12, *12
Stanford Road 73
Stanhope Avenue 63
Stanhope cinema 91-92, *92
Stanhope Road 86
Station Parade 109
Stephens, Henry C. 26, 27-28, 32
Stephens, Rev. Henry 91, 96
Stephens Memorial Hall 91, *91, 97
Sternberg Centre 61
Strathearn, Totteridge Green 135
Strawberry Brook 62, 85
Strawberry Vale 9, 51, *51
Studio Cole 109
Summerlee estate *45
Summers Lane 69, 70, 91
Summerside School 69
Surveyor of Highways 22
Sutcliffe & Butler 63
Swan & Pyramids 12, 104, *105
Swan Lane 110
Swan Lane recreation ground 109
Sweet's nursery 119-120
Sweets Way 120
Swimming Pools 59, 65, *65, *66
Sycamore Close 8

Sydney Rad 87
Sydney Road School 87
Sylvester Road 50

TALLY HO coach 12, *12
Tally Ho Corner 93, *93, 93, *93
Tass 123
Telford, Thomas 11
Templars Crescent 28
Temple Avenue 127
Temple Croft Field 26
Terrace House, Woodside Lane 104
Territorial Army 64
Tesco's 32
Tewart, Edward 88
Thackrah Close 50
Thatcher, Margaret 33, 50
Thomas More Way 54
Thorley, Joseph 32
Thorowgood, John 134
Three Horse Shoes, Whetstone 115, *118
Three Horse Shoes, Totteridge 136-137
Thurlestone Avenue 82
Tillingham Way 90
Torrington Arms 11, *13, *100, 101
Torrington Park 16, *17, 101
Totteridge 7, 9, 129-139
Totteridge and Whetstone Station 16, 120
Totteridge Green 135-137
Totteridge Lane 114, 120, *121
Totteridge Manor Association 135
Totteridge Manor Farm 134
Totteridge Park (house) 134
Totteridge Park 129
Towers, The, Bishop's Avenue 40
Traffic lights 73
Trams 14-15, *15, *38, 92, *94
Trinity Avenue 55
Trinity Road 55, *55
Triumph pub 70
Trolleybuses 14, 15, *15
Tromer, John 30
Tromers Street 30
Tudor School 59
Turle, Dr. 104
Turner family 33
Turnpikes 10-11, *108
Tyrhtel, Bishop of Hereford 9

UNITED Dairies 26
United Estates and Investment Co. 86
Uxber, Richard 106

VARDON, Harry 139, *139
Vaughan, James and Ernest 28
Ventnor Drive 90
Ventris, Revd Henry 114
Vicarage, Totteridge 131
Victoria Avenue 29
Victoria Park 36, *36, 88
Village Road 24

WAITROSE 12
Wakeling Moor 8
Walfield 128, 8128

Walfield Avenue 128
Walfield House 128
Walks, The 43
Warnham Road 74
Waterlow, George 124
Waugh, Benjamin 86
Weatherhead, Douglas 86
Weld, Mary 60
Wells, Ald. Vyvyan 23
Wells, Henry 23
Wentworth estate 32
Wentworth Hall 33, *33, *34
Wentworth Lodge 32
Wentworth Park 23
West Heath, Hampstead 7
Westbury Road 90
Westminster Freehold Land Society 87
Wheeler, Frederick 33, 68
Whetstone & Highgate Turnpike Trust 10-11
Whetstone 106-128
Whetstone Freehold Estate Co. 123
Whetstone House 120, 128
Whetstone Place 117, *120
Whetstone Society 122, 128
Whetstone stone *113
Whetstone Street 18
White House 74
White Lion *10, 12, 37, *37
White, Rev. Thomas Reader 20
Whiteley, William 56
Wilkinson, Revd 134
Williams, J.L. 130
Williamson, James 29, 30, 88
Wilmot Close 50, *50
Wimbush, Samuel 90
Windermere Avenue 28, 63
Windsor Castle pub 43
Wingate football club 65
Women's Land Army 134
Wood, John 134
Woodberry Grove 92
Woodbridge School 90
Woodcroft, Totteridge Green 136
Woodhouse 9, 98, *98
Woodhouse College 98
Woodhouse Road 14, 21, 71, *97, 98
Woodhouse School 99
Woodlands 110, 111
Woodside Assembly Rooms 101
Woodside estate 113
Woodside Grange 104
Woodside Lane 104
Woodside Park *89
Woodside Park Road 101
Woodside Park station *17, 99, *99
Woodward, J. 32
Workhouses 41-42
Wright, George 98
Wright, Miss Blanch 67
Wright-Kingsford Home 67, *68, 88
Wykeham Rise, Totteridge 133

Wyrhales, Isabella 122